# BACK I. STEAM

*The Downpatrick and County Down Railway from 1982*

## Gerry Cochrane

*Foreword by WF Gillespie OBE*

This book is dedicated to all those unsung volunteers who, with their hard work and dedication, were instrumental in preserving our railway heritage for future generations.
Also to those individuals and organisations whose generous contributions, both financial and in kind, have helped to make dreams come true.

First Edition
First impression

© Gerry Cochrane
and Colourpoint Books
Newtownards 2009

Designed by Colourpoint Books, Newtownards
Printed by GPS Colour Graphics Ltd, Belfast

ISBN  978 1 906578 29 9

Gerry Cochrane was born in 1935 within sight and sound of the BCDR. Since early childhood, he has had a strong interest in railways. His final thesis in architecture was based on the study of Working Railway Museums, researched in both Great Britain and Europe. He joined the South Eastern Education and Library Board and became Senior Architect. In 1982 he began a process which has resulted in the return of steam to Downpatrick. The onset of ME brought his professional career to a premature end in 1991, but Gerry continued with the development of the railway museum until retirement from management in 2004. His activities are now confined to vintage carriage restoration.

**Photo Credits**
All photographs, unless otherwise credited, are by the author.

Colourpoint Books
Colourpoint House
Jubilee Business Park
Jubilee Road
NEWTOWNARDS
County Down
Northern Ireland
BT23 4YH
Tel: (028) 9182 6339
Fax: (028) 9182 1900
E-mail: info@colourpoint.co.uk
Web-site: www.colourpoint.co.uk

**Cover Photographs**

*Front cover:* Ex-GS&WR 0-6-0T No 90 runs round at Inch Abbey on 17 March 2008.

*Norman Johnston*

*Rear cover, top:* O&K 0-4-0T No 3 crosses the Quoile bridge towards Inch Abbey on a train from Downpatrick on 1 May 2006.

*Wilson Adams*

*Rear cover, bottom:* The BCDR Royal Saloon of 1897.

*Drawing by the author*

# CONTENTS

# FOREWORD

*by W F Gillespie OBE*

When a few of us met in Denvir's Hotel on a bleak winter night to discuss the possibility of a preserved railway scheme at Downpatrick, it was somewhat unreal, and perhaps none of us – except Gerry Cochrane – really expected that our dreams would ever be realised.

As described in this book, many obstacles were encountered and there were times when most of us – except Gerry Cochrane – were prepared to give up. However, he is made of sterner stuff, and always sought and found a way through the difficulties. It was my pleasure and privilege to help clear some of the obstacles, particularly in the early days, and in the process, I came to admire the tenacity and determination of Gerry and other colleagues who joined in the enterprise over the years. It has also been my pleasure to develop a lasting friendship with Gerry and his wife, typical of the many friendships which arise from working on railway activities.

I well recall the thrill of first seeing ex-CIÉ diesel locomotive No 421 pulling a restored goods van from our Station to the Loop. This and many later sights on our Railway have brought thrills and satisfaction to me and thousands of others.

This delightful book will be of much interest to all who have an interest in railways, especially the much revered Belfast and County Down Railway – the BCDR. Downpatrick and County Down Railway is a worthy successor which could not have been achieved without the input of Gerry Cochrane.

# INTRODUCTION

I have been asked many times over the past few years to write an account of the history of the Downpatrick Railway Museum for inclusion in its archives. Two people in particular made the initial suggestion, Bill Gillespie and Ciaran McAteer, both of whom were, along with myself and others, Directors on the Board in the earlier years. I received further encouragement and the suggestion of writing a book from my wife, Roisin, as well as my two sons, Niall and Feargal. Sometimes I felt that they had my mortality in mind which was a bit disconcerting. However, I realised that unless I took their advice a lot of the early history of this project would eventually be lost, and so I agreed to do it.

"How will I start?" "Where do I begin"? These thoughts were to preoccupy my mind for some time. I thought about the numerous times during lunch-breaks at the railway other volunteers would ask questions about its history. "Where did the old carriages come from?" "How did they get to Downpatrick?" "What was the initial site like when I first came to view it?" The realisation dawned on me that a considerable length of time had passed since it all began and newer members had no idea how and why it had all happened.

I have drawn mainly from memory of significant events dating back over the past twenty-five years, supported by reference to correspondence files, minutes of Directors' and Management Committee meetings, press cuttings, together with our Railway Society's publications. Anecdotes relating to particular events help to convey some of the emotions and experiences which are inevitable in a voluntary organisation of this type.

Teamwork on the part of our volunteers has resulted in the restoration of train services to this part of the BCDR, culminating with the first train ever to arrive at Inch Abbey. Limitations on space made it necessary for me to concentrate on specific activities from inception in 1982 to the opening of the Inch Abbey Extension in 2004, though some more recent pictures have been included.

I am confident that this book could not have been written without the practical help of my wife, Roisin, who provided much-needed encouragement when at times my resolve to complete the task hit the buffers. I am grateful to her for her continuous support, patience and encouragement.

My grateful thanks are due to Michael Collins, an informed colleague over many years, for undertaking the tiresome task of proof reading the manuscript and I welcome his insightful and useful comments.

Lastly I would like to thank Norman Johnston of Colourpoint Books for his encouragement and enthusiasm during the preparation of this book.

*Spring 2009*

# CHAPTER 1

# BACKGROUND

"How did you get interested in railways?" This question is one I am frequently asked and which is impossible to answer in a few words.

I was born within the sound and smell of the Belfast & County Down Railway (BCDR), about half a mile from the Neill's Hill railway station in East Belfast. This was the third station on the BCDR main line out of Belfast, which served Downpatrick, Newcastle and Donaghadee.

From Belfast the route had a steady climb up to Bloomfield station, under Sandown Road bridge and finally through a deep cutting as the track approached Neill's Hill station.

At night, when in bed, I could hear trains working hard as they climbed up the bank from Bloomfield.

Sometimes I could also hear trains shunting and whistling as they went about their work. On looking back, I think these sounds must have come from the BCDR depot at Queen's Quay in Belfast, some three miles away.

From the station a narrow cinder footpath was provided for the convenience of passengers living in the new housing development where I also lived. Although within the outer suburbs of Belfast, this path had a very rural atmosphere, providing a lovely walk, as well as being an excellent vantage point for anyone viewing trains.

My first encounter with a steam engine at Neill's Hill occurred when I was about two years old. Mother and I, with my sister in a pram, had probably been out for a walk. My first impression of this monster breathing smoke and steam was so exciting and made a lasting impression on me.

In 1941, my primary school in Ballyhackamore was destroyed during the German air-raid at Easter. Fortunately, I was not in it at the time as the raid took place during the night. Instead, I was sheltering under the stairs at my

home in Holland Gardens. Like most children in Belfast at that time, my sister and I were eventually evacuated to the country for a few years to escape any danger.

On my return to Belfast I was sent to a primary school in Oxford Street which was situated near the centre of Belfast. Although the school building itself was Dickensian, having only a back alley as a playground, I discovered there was a bonus to this arrangement.

Just around the corner from the school was a shop selling, among other things, train sets and I can still clearly remember displayed in the window, a *Duchess of Atholl* electric passenger set. Every day on my way home from school, I would drool over this beautiful model, until one day, sadly, I noticed it was gone.

I already had an 'O' gauge clockwork Hornby train set which comprised an LMS 4-4-2 tank locomotive, a few wagons and an oval track. It had been supplied to me by Santa Claus at Christmas 1943. Some years later I discovered that my parents had acquired it second-hand from the 'for sale' section of the Belfast Telegraph, the local evening newspaper.

This train set was very limited in that there were no points, passenger carriages, signals or the other accessories that make an interesting layout. When I grumbled about this, I was politely informed that I was lucky to get what I had, as there was a war on and Santa had some difficulty getting children toys.

The journey home from my new school gave me some interesting transport choices. I could take the tram or, more appealing on a good day, take the Cherryvalley bus, which was a Guy single-deck utility noisy bone shaker, but it would let me off at Neill's Hill station with the ensuing pleasant half mile walk home alongside the railway.

Sometimes, if I had a ha'penny, a farthing or some nails

| STATIONS. | MAIN LINE TRAINS—WEEK-DAYS. | | | | | | | | | | | | | | | | | | | | | |
|---|---|---|---|---|---|---|---|---|---|---|---|---|---|---|---|---|---|---|---|---|---|---|

*(Down trains timetable — main line week-days)*

| STATIONS | MAIN LINE TRAINS—WEEK-DAYS—Contd. | | | | | | | | | | | | | | | | | | | | | |
|---|---|---|---|---|---|---|---|---|---|---|---|---|---|---|---|---|---|---|---|---|---|---|

*Above:* BCDR timetable 1 October 1925. Down trains

distribution of wildlife as they were a natural habitat largely undisturbed by cultivation and insecticides. They thus became wildlife highways.

On one occasion, during a butterfly expedition along this path, my thoughts were rudely disturbed when I nearly tripped on a bomb. It looked to me to be fairly new and had not exploded. It was about 12 inches long with impressive fins. Carefully, I retreated and ran to Neill's Hill station to tell the station-master. For some reason it was the signalman who came to inspect the object. I could not believe my eyes when he walked forward and stooped to pick it up. At this point I fled in horror and ran all the way home, expecting to hear of his eventual demise.

The main highlight of 1945 was going on holiday to Killough where we stayed on a working farm about half a mile from the village. With my mother, father and sister we walked to Neill's Hill station to wait for the Downpatrick train. As is always the case for me, the anticipation of the train journey was the best part of the holiday. Suddenly, the bell rang in the station. The signalman, whom I was glad to see was still alive, would come down from his house and open the crossing gates for the train. A few minutes later the signal arm would drop with a 'clonk' and we knew that the train was now approaching.

On our arrival at Downpatrick, we had to change to the Ardglass train which was already patiently sitting waiting for us at its own platform

in my pocket, this was a convenient place to slip under the wire fence and put them on the track, although it usually took about half an hour to find them after the train had passed. This was to be my first experience of 'cold forging'.

I remember reading some years ago that railway routes throughout the country played an important role in the

*Right:* BCDR 4-4-2T No 1 departs from Downpatrick, prtobably in the late 1940s. Note the water tower, now replicated in the new station.

*Eric Russell, courtesy London & North Western Railway Society*

***Right:*** NIRTB buses dominate this scene outside Downpatrick station in the late 1940s.

and it was soon on its way, passing the Loop Platform, Ballynoe and then Killough where we alighted. This was the penultimate station on the Ardglass Branch. Killough is a small picturesque sea-side village with a harbour but its most interesting attraction for me then was its smithy. This Aladdin's cave was sandwiched between single storey cottages in the centre of the main street. To witness the red hot iron being forged with the associated smoke and steam was fascinating for a young boy to watch.

Although my memory of this journey is still quite good, I do not recall any other passengers on the train. A sign of things to come perhaps, as within five years the whole of the BCDR, with the exception of the Bangor branch, would be closed. One regular visitor to Neill's Hill Station was our neighbour's dog, who would wait on the platform for his master to come home for his lunch on the 12.50 train from Belfast. It is interesting to note that the journey from Queens Quay to Neill's Hill at that time was seven minutes while to-day the same journey would take fifteen minutes at best.

The closure was a traumatic experience for the local population, as the railway played a large part in their lives. For the employees, their way of life had been killed off and the resulting loss of jobs added to the gloom.

I can also recall around this time my parents buying me a set of 'Children's Encyclopaedia' which consisted of twelve volumes, probably given to me with the intention of furthering my education. The main feature of interest which I can still vividly remember was a full page display in wonderful colour of four express locomotives of the main English railways. These were an LNER A4 *Mallard*, an LMS 'Coronation' Pacific, a GWR 'King' and an SR 'Merchant Navy'. It must be 60 years since I last saw this illustration, but it is clearly etched on my memory.

A visit with my father in 1946 to the Model Engineers' Exhibition in the YMCA in Belfast made a profound impression on me. I had no idea that ordinary people could make such wonderful models and I was determined that one day I would build a working steam locomotive.

Another memorable occasion was a visit to the Belfast Corporation tramway workshops at Sandy Row in Belfast when I had the good fortune to be there to witness the fitting of a steel tyre to a tram wheel. The method was fascinating. In the centre of the workshop floor a group of men were gathered around a steel tyre which was surrounded by fire. When the tyre was red hot the centre portion of the wheel was lowered into the expanded tyre which was then quenched with water. All these procedures were very dramatic and instructive for a ten-year-old boy. Already, my fascination with fire and steam was becoming apparent.

## Intermission

Quite a long period elapsed before I could fulfil my ambition to start work on a steam locomotive and in the meantime, horse drawn carts, trams and trolleybuses were to disappear off the streets of Belfast. It was a time, too, when I began my future career in architecture.

In 1960, I purchased a site in East Belfast with the intention of building a house in time for my forthcoming wedding. This elevated and mature site was originally the croquet lawn belonging to a grand house which had been built for Wolff of Harland & Wolff, the Belfast shipbuilders. What an unbelievable oasis I had found for my future home, with a panoramic view over the city. Naturally, I designed and built the house myself with some help from direct labour and of course from my future wife. I well remember while working on the roof, the grand view I had of the P&O Liner, *Canberra*, which was being constructed in Harland & Wolff's at the same time and which was to become Belfast's future pride and joy. I also made sure I would have a small workshop when the house was completed, judging that it might come in useful some day.

Before too long and with wedding nuptials now successfully over, the time had come for me to realise my dream. I was now in a position to make a start at long last on the construction of my first coal-fired model steam locomotive. My final choice, after due consideration, was an LNER A3 Pacific in 3½" (89mm) track gauge.

First, I had to obtain copies of the original works drawings from British Railways in Doncaster in order to incorporate as much authentic detail as possible, the basic constructional drawings being supplied by Clarkson of York. As I had no engineering experience, I had to learn the different processes as I went along. There were so many different metals involved, such as mild steel, stainless steel, cast iron, brass, bronze gun-metal and copper, to name but a few, all with different uses and working properties, all of which had to be mastered over a period of fifteen years to enable the model to be completed to my satisfaction. The magazine *Model Engineer* was the source of all my information and I eagerly looked forward to it every month.

Unfortunately, by the late seventies the 'Troubles' were at their height and I found that, with two teenage sons, East Belfast was not the most comfortable location in which to live safely.

We therefore made the decision to move to the country,

***Above:*** The author's model LNER A3 Pacific under construction.

***Above:*** The completed model.

just a few miles outside Downpatrick in County Down. Despite some understandable worries and reservations on my wife's part, this move proved to be a big success for everyone concerned. It was definitely a case of the cloud having a silver lining. However, it did mean building another house, or more accurately, the restoration of a ruined cottage of which I had fond memories when visiting as a very young child with my family. By this time, too, I was working for the South Eastern Education & Library Board (SEELB) where I eventually obtained the position of Senior Architect. This move was to prove significant in the years to come in helping to shape the Downpatrick Railway Project.

## Something Stirring

I had become acquainted with the late Bob Beggs of the Ulster Folk and Transport Museum (UFTM) at Cultra while researching a working railway museum for my final thesis in architecture. Bob was curator as well as a well known model engineer, chiefly responsible for the acquisition of most of the railway exhibits which are now in the in the UFTM.

My contact with Bob, together with my research into working railway museums in Great Britain, mainland Europe and the USA, led me to realise that our local railway heritage was in danger of being lost. While the Railway Preservation Society of Ireland (RPSI) was doing tremendous work in restoring and operating locomotives, there was no standard gauge working railway museum on the island of Ireland. I felt something had to be done as a matter of urgency and so began to dream.

There are many interesting aspects to railways of the steam era, such as locomotives, carriages, track, architecture and civil engineering, the obvious star of the show being the steam locomotive. This man-made invention suddenly comes to life once the fire is lit and behaves like a living creature. If it has to work hard pulling a heavy freight train up a steep gradient the whole countryside through which it journey's will know about it. On the other hand, if it moves without any load, it just saunters along the track

with a gentle hiss of steam. You could be standing beside it and hardly hear it. Each locomotive, too, had its own individual character, good, bad or indifferent. They were all individuals, just like their drivers. There is an indescribable fascination with a large precision machine moving through the countryside, over viaducts, through cuttings, even over mountains, guided with great precision by the track. It is without question, 'poetry in motion'.

Carriages too, especially those in operation during the great days of steam, were also works of art. There were so many different types, from the common suburban vehicle to the grandeur of a Royal Saloon. These all had one thing in common, ie they were all built to the highest standards of workmanship and were made with the best of available materials. Each railway company had its own livery and they vied with each other to be the most splendid.

There is nothing sadder than the sight of an abandoned railway, with rusty rails, derelict stations, signal cabins and weeds growing up between the rotting timber sleepers, the only trains being ghost trains or those in one's imagination.

There is a tremendous urge in anyone who loves railways to try and turn the clock back and recreate, to some extent, the magic of the former days.

This urge is usually satisfied in most enthusiasts by building a small scale model railway layout, well within the ability of anyone to achieve. At the other extreme, there are those, judged by some to be slightly insane, who are not satisfied with anything less than the full size restoration. This 'love affair' should help to explain the passions, dedication and determination of the animal species generally best known as a 'railway enthusiast'.

*Photos below from the Aubrey Ray collection*

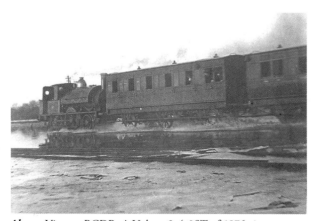

***Above:*** Vintage BCDR. A Vulcan 2-4-0ST of 1876 vintage departs from Downpatrick in the early 1900s.

***Above:*** Probably on the same day, a small 4-4-2T is shunting a horsebox and van. The Quoile has burst its banks!

# CHAPTER 2
# BIG IDEAS

During 1982, I became aware of a restoration project being proposed in the Ballynahinch area and on making further inquires obtained a copy of a feasibility study prepared by the Belfast & County Down Railway Museum Trust (BCDRMT).

With my previous research into working railway museums still fresh in my mind, I spent a pleasant few weeks looking at all the locations listed in the study. An unexpected opportunity led to a visit to Downpatrick where my son Niall was to take his driving test. With an hour to kill, I decided to have a look at the site of the abandoned railway which had served the market town. I was most impressed with the whole area and could immediately see the potential for a very interesting working railway museum.

*Above:* View from carpark looking towards the DOE roads compound; now station building and workshop.

The track bed in the immediate Downpatrick area was still intact and with an interesting triangular layout. It was also completely unspoilt by development and identical to its appearance of one hundred years earlier. In addition, the land was owned by Lord Henry Dunleath, whose interest in railways was well known and who could be expected to be favourably disposed to such a development.

The main advantages of this location were that its terminus would be virtually in the centre of Downpatrick, within walking distance of the proposed Down County Museum and with direct access to a large existing free DOE car park. The decision of the BCDRMT to opt for Ballynahinch was therefore very surprising.

*Above:* Main approach to Downpatrick, looking north.

*Above:* Looking towards Downpatrick from the 'Loop'.

Some of the original railway buildings still remained, including the Loop Platform and its canopy. This was an island platform with an overall roof supported on typical Victorian iron columns having scroll iron work brackets and cast iron shell bases. This particular platform was most unusual in that it was only accessible by rail. To the west, beyond the Loop, the original branch line for Ardglass left the main line in the direction of Ballynoe, a few miles further on. The whole of the original station complex there, including road crossing gates, station house, goods shed and signal cabin were completely intact, although the station house was now in use as a dwelling.

*Above:* Ballynoe station and goods shed.

*Above:* Killough goods shed.

Further on, Killough Station and goods shed were also in their original state although converted into domestic accommodation, while Ardglass station building was unoccupied and in the early stages of dereliction.

The Downpatrick location, therefore, in my opinion, offered many more attractions and had the possibility of a link to the picturesque fishing port of Ardglass, nine miles from Downpatrick.

*Above:* Ardglass station.

I was convinced that the BCDRMT was missing a great opportunity and I became determined to bring this to the attention of interested authorities, although I had no intention at that time of becoming personally involved.

My views as to the form that this particular 'working railway museum' should take were clearly defined. They were to endeavour to recreate the Edwardian era, which was the pinnacle of the steam age and characterised the BCDR. When the railway closed it was still operating with locomotives which were designed in 1901 and with six-wheel carriages which were built just after the turn of the century, technically Victorian of course but built and operated during the Edwardian period.

I envisaged that this would not be a museum in the traditional form, ie static, but would be 'alive' with all the original carriages restored to working order, enabling visitors to experience travel of that period. An important aspect would be that visitors would also be able to witness restoration work in progress and perhaps even become involved themselves. I also envisaged that this would be a railway museum built and operated almost exclusively by volunteer labour but with a significant input by ACE[1] workers to assist with the construction and eventual maintenance. This then was the general outline of what I wished to see and felt sure that it would have maximum appeal to local people as well as tourists.

By 1982 it was nearly too late to save the important elements of our local railway heritage. I was realistic enough to realise that it was going to be a mammoth task to get together a representative collection of original carriages of the period. Some had survived on farms where they had been purchased from the railway company for use as chicken houses, though now, unfortunately, minus their underframes and wheels. A few Edwardian carriages also survived in southern Ireland in the ownership of CIÉ, the attraction of these being that they were complete, with underframes and wheels.

Locomotives were going to be a different proposition altogether, as all of the BCDR engines, with one exception, had been cut up for scrap. The exception referred to was BCDR locomotive No 30, now secure in the UFTM and most unlikely to be allowed to 'escape' to Downpatrick.

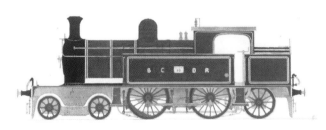

BELFAST & COUNTY DOWN RAILWAY NO.30

I can recall a visit I made to Maysfields marshalling yard in East Belfast around 1963, and how very sad I'd been to see all the redundant steam locomotives assembled there waiting to be scrapped. There were locomotives from the LMS(NCC), and GNRI, at least thirty locomotives in all. We were just twenty years too late and would obviously have to be satisfied with 'foreign' motive power.

## The Master Plan

However, undaunted, I set about thinking about all the possibilities with Downpatrick as the starting point and Ardglass as a possible long term and attractive destination. This would have provided a train trip of about nine miles. In addition, Ballynoe and Killough were attractive, unspoilt, intermediate stations. In order to make this ambitious scheme manageable it would need to be considered in three phases.

***Phase One*** would comprise of the reinstatement of track from Market Street, Downpatrick to the Ballydugan Road, including the Loop Platform and north to the Quoile River. (this was later amended to include Ballydugan Mill and Inch Abbey)

***Phase Two*** would take the railway across the Ballydugan Road, past Down Racecourse and up the one in fifty gradient to Ballynoe.

***Phase Three*** would continue to Killough and Ardglass.

I described my ideas to my long-suffering wife, expecting to get a short reply, but was surprised by her positive reaction and her suggestion that I explore the possibilities of support within the area. I felt I had just passed my first hurdle.

## Local Reaction

In addition to my interest in railway heritage, as a resident of the area I was very much aware of the chronic unemployment situation in Down District at that time and considered that the proposed scheme would benefit tourism and provide a boost for local employment.

This gave me confidence to approach the former Chairman of Down District Council (DDC), Mr Eddie McGrady, to assess the Council's attitude to the general idea of a working railway museum, as well as his own reaction to my proposal. His immediate response was favourable and he asked me to attend a meeting with himself and the Council's Director of Tourism, Bryan Coburn.

At this meeting, Mr Coburn was able to provide us with the latest update of the situation regarding the BCDRMT and thought that our proposal deserved further consideration. It was agreed that Mr McGrady would make an announcement in the local press in order to gauge public reaction. The press release was as follows;

### *Plans for Railway from Downpatrick*[2]

*Alternative plans have been put forward this week for a £½ million pound scheme to construct a Working Railway Museum between Downpatrick and Ardglass.*

*The museum would be based in Downpatrick and if given the green light, would be the first standard gauge preserved working railway in Ireland.* Down Recorder 26/08/82

*Basically the scheme being promoted by former Down District Council chairman, Mr Eddie McGrady and local railway enthusiast, Mr Gerry Cochrane, would be in three phases and would eventually link Downpatrick with Ardglass by rail. The first phase of the project would involve constructing two miles of track from Market Street in Downpatrick, the site of the former station, to the disused bridge at Ballydugan Road.*

*The second and third ..........*

*Mr McGrady is promoting this new scheme as an alternative to the Ballynahinch Junction project put forward by the Belfast & County Down Railway Museum Trust last year because he feels it has a higher tourist potential........*

This publicity, coming out of the blue, caused quite a stir among the general public, particularly among some landowners and residents of original railway property who were understandably annoyed about not having been previously consulted. Others, however, offered their co-operation, while some scoffed at the idea and dismissed the proposal as 'pie in the sky'.

The reaction from the BCDRMT was immediate and also very supportive. They indicated their interest and at their AGM in October 1982, by a unanimous decision, voted to abandon the Saintfield/Ballynahinch scheme in favour of Downpatrick. A quotation from its Chairman at the time reads - "I am very much in favour of Mr McGrady's proposals and personally believe that this site would be the best in Northern Ireland for a working railway museum".[3]

Perhaps the most important result of this publicity for me and one which was to have a significant effect on the success of the scheme was that I received a telephone call and offer of support from Colonel Bill Gillespie OBE. I had previously met him during the conversion of Castlewellan Market House for use as a library. He was the Managing Director of John Sinton Ltd, the main contractor, while I was the Senior Architect with the SEELB.

I had no idea of his interest in railways and his offer of help, therefore, came totally out of the blue, was timely and very much appreciated. I did not realise then, the magnitude and importance of this help, both advisory and financial, which was to be given so generously during the following years.

Another influential local person who agreed to help at this time was a local landowner, the late Patrick Forde. I well remember entering Seaforde Demesne to meet Paddy, and while on my way up the long, tree lined avenue to the great house, wondering what type of reception I could expect, as I was a complete stranger to him at that time.

I explained the project in detail and with the knowledge he had already gleaned from the local press, I was agreeably surprised when he confirmed that he would be glad to lend his name and join the promotion team.

During these early years I had become acquainted with Dr Brian Turner, recently appointed Curator of the new Down Museum. At that time, his office was located in a small house opposite the former County Gaol where he was in the process of trying to get the County Museum off the ground. I used to call with him from time to time and discuss my own ideas and was very grateful for his help and advice, especially when we were involved in the formal setting up of our own museum.

It was the reaction of people such as I have just mentioned as well as many others, which gave me encouragement to continue my efforts in this ever expanding and demanding project, although I was getting more deeply involved than I had initially intended.

## Railway Promoters

The first meeting to discuss the reopening of the Downpatrick section of the BCDR was held in the historic Denvir's Hotel, on 13 January 1983. Unlike railway promoters of the 19th century, the individuals present[4] were not interested in making vast fortunes, but instead were prepared to give up an inordinate amount of their free time over the coming years to a project which they all regarded as worthwhile.

The main objective of this meeting was to consider

the proposal and map out the way forward. Bill offered to prepare a draft constitution and float the idea with Lord Dunleath. I was given two weeks to prepare a costed feasibility study.

Bill obtained a favourable response from Lord Dunleath who indicated that he would be more than happy to make available all the land required for Phase One, owned by Dunleath Estates Ltd, on the former BCDR. He commented that there was nothing he would like more than to see the Downpatrick to Ardglass line re-opened, the only proviso being that they would want to retain access to the Cathedral lands and that we should undertake liability for all fencing.

His interest in the environment was illustrated by his desire that the surrounding marshes should remain as a wild life reserve and he recalled that when the BCDR was operating, wild life did not seem to be disturbed by the activity of the trains. I am not so sure about that, having read about the exploits of former engine drivers as well as signalmen, some of whom took pot shots at ducks and other game. This type of behaviour would, of course, not be tolerated on our restored railway!

Interestingly, he also recalled, that when the Belfast to Newcastle line closed and the track bed was offered to the riparian owners, he urged his father to buy the track and signalling equipment in case the line was ever to be re-opened at some time in the future.

His father declined, pointing out firstly, that it would greatly add to the purchase price, and secondly, the disused track would soon deteriorate without regular maintenance. There was also the question of economics, as the Estate would be responsible for all the fencing as well as being liable for any accidents which might occur. Lastly, he saw no prospect of the railway ever being re-opened as a viable enterprise.

By this time Down District Council's Tourism and Recreation Committee had approved our project and a follow up meeting with all concerned, including the RPSI and BCDRMT was held again in Denvir's Hotel to appoint a committee to take the project forward.[5]

Shortly after this meeting, to our surprise and dismay, the BCDRMT publicly expounded on television the merits of the Ballynahinch scheme and seemed to have a lot of support from some of the Ballynahinch councillors.

This development came as a bombshell and caused much consternation and upset within our committee. It was with great disappointment that we subsequently learned that the BCDRMT had reverted to its original project at Ballynahinch Junction. Things did not look good for us as the scheme now appeared to be coming under political influences. However, we had confidence in the merits of our proposals and decided to press on regardless.

This latest development put Down District Council in a quandary because they were now faced with two different schemes within their District and had to make a decision as to which, if any, they would support.

Bryan Coburn reported to his Recreation and Tourist Committee that a requirement of the Department of Economic Development (DED) was that such a scheme would require the support of the Railway Preservation Society of Ireland, due to their wealth of experience as well as the potential use of their excellent repair facilities at Whitehead. He went on to inform his Committee that the RPSI had formally confirmed that they would not support the Ballynahinch Junction Scheme but considered that, on the contrary, the Downpatrick/Ardglass scheme had a real possibility of becoming a major attraction.

At this stage we were informed that the Northern Ireland Tourist Board, together with the DED, were making it very clear that they would support only one working railway museum in Northern Ireland and that any financial support would be restricted accordingly. They were aware by this stage that three different railway schemes were being proposed. These were at Scarva/Banbridge, Ballynahinch Junction and Downpatrick, although the Scarva scheme by this time was on the verge of being abandoned.

By this stage, it was becoming clear that we would soon need the services of a solicitor and Ciaran McAteer's name was mentioned as a person who had been involved with the RPSI on their Scarva–Banbridge branch-line proposal. I arranged to meet him and can still remember my embarrassment on approaching his office to request his help. What would he think of this hare-brained scheme?

My concern was to prove unfounded, for on entering his office it became obvious from some photographs adorning his walls that I was on home ground and had a kindred soul in front of me. I found Ciaran's interest in the project very encouraging and his unstinting help and guidance has continued to the present day

The year 1983 was an important milestone for us, when the RPSI gave a conditional offer of support. They made it clear, however, that their main ambition, understandably, was to have a rail connected branch line of their own and should such an opportunity present itself in future, it was felt that the Society would have to support such a scheme.

The follow-up to all that was that the Recreation and Tourist Committee recommended that representatives from both local schemes should be invited to attend their offices at the next Council meeting to explain their individual schemes.

Submissions were made by our delegation[6] following that of the BCDRMT. After a nail-biting wait, we were told the outcome was that the Council had adopted the Downpatrck/Ardglass scheme in principle, subject to it obtaining grant-aid.

It was now up to DDC to decide on the level of financial support they were prepared to give, a difficult decision for councillors, as they were unfamiliar with the subject of railways and what it involved. To be faced with a scheme of such magnitude, the first of its kind on the island of Ireland, and also at a time of financial pressure, would require great courage and imagination on their part.

On the other hand, the degree of personal commitment on the part of the promoters was obvious and the opportunity for Down District to acquire such a unique tourist attraction, which would be built, operated and maintained entirely by volunteers, (with, we hoped a little help from ACE workers) was a prize worthy of their serious consideration.

## The Downpatrick Agreement

The eventual outcome was that Down District Council agreed to be responsible for the following in relation to Phase One. Subsequent phases would be considered in due course.

## Phase One

DDC would be responsible for the acquisition of land from Market Street to the Ballydugan Road and to the Quoile River, including the Loop Platform, and the sub-leasing of the land to the Railway Company.

DDC would also be responsible for capital works: ie station, workshop, Loop Platform and Magnus's Grave platform together with building insurance; also the preparation of the track bed, and the refurbishment of

bridge No 163. The introduction of an ACE Scheme would also be the responsibility of DDC.

The Railway Company would be responsible for the acquisition, restoration and operation of carriages and locomotives, including the operation of the railway on a self-financing basis once completed and to have the museum open for a minimum of 60 days per year.

The year 1983 was proving to be significant with the arrangement of another important meeting involving most of the prominent names[7] in the local railway preservation movement. This was held in Downpatrick Library with the aim of generating additional support and appointing a formal committee to drive the project forward on a professional basis. The outcome was encouraging in many respects, chiefly because of the positive attitude taken by Bryan Coburn on behalf of DDC when he reiterated the Council's decision to acquire land and provide capital funding subject to grant aid, for such a scheme.

In the strength of all that, we went ahead and staged an exhibition in Downpatrick Library with the purpose of explaining the aims and objectives of our proposal to the general public. During the formal opening to invited guests one rather irate landowner tried to gate-crash the occasion but the situation was saved by the Librarian on duty, Mrs Muriel Major, who firmly but politely ejected the offender from the premises, with the advice that the occasion was private and that he should make his protest at a later date.

Despite this, the success of this exhibition, which was open to the public for three days, went beyond our expectations and resulted in a very strong management committee[8] being set up. In addition, the public reaction gave us further stimulus to proceed with renewed vigour.

For the next few months, much time was taken up in intense discussions with the RPSI, NITB, UFTM and the DED regarding our ability to acquire a steam locomotive, a key to further progress and described in detail in Chapter 4.

In September 1984 a public meeting was arranged in Downpatrick Leisure Centre to develop public support and enrol volunteers in the fledgling Downpatrick & Ardglass Railway Society. There was an excellent response which resulted in a core of working members enrolling, the majority of whom are still working as hard as ever to this day.

One thing I have learned about railway preservation is that a surprise of some kind is always lurking behind the door. On this particular occasion, just before this meeting

***Above:*** Gerry Cochrane, Brian Quinn, Eddie McGready, Robert Edwards, Paddy Forde, Bill Gillespie, Pat Magee

commenced, someone handed me a copy of that day's Down Recorder, the front page headline read -

### "RAIL LINK STOPPED IN ITS TRACKS"

Not a very promising beginning, but it proved to have no effect on the enthusiasm of those present. The article referred to a campaign by most of the local landowners who were affected by our proposal and were aggrieved because they had not been consulted beforehand. We were told to stay off their land in future. We tried to placate them by informing them that we were concentrating on Phase 1, over which there would be no land contention.

Nevertheless, it was considered important that the adverse criticism should be dealt with and that a press statement should be issued to coincide with a letter from myself as Secretary, to each of the concerned landowners which read as follows:-.

Downpatrick & Ardglass Railway Society

Dear ………..Landowner          19th November 1984

Re:- Working Railway Museum

Due to the obvious concern of landowners, I have been asked by our Committee to write to all concerned in order to allay fears and to correct misunderstandings which have arisen.

Phase One of the scheme which has already started is regarded as a pilot scheme to test the degree of support and to gauge the ability of local people to make it a successful operation.

Only then could meaningful discussions take place with those affected regarding the subsequent phases.

A number of serious misunderstandings appear to have arisen regarding the original railway buildings some of which are now in residential use.

It was never that those residents should vacate their homes. Farmers who have reclaimed the track bed for agricultural or other purposes would obviously have to be accommodated and their needs for access fully recognised.

Although formal detailed negotiations are some years off, members of our committee would welcome discussions with individual owners in the intervening period should this be requested.

Yours sincerely,
E.P.G.Cochrane.
Secretary

This was followed by personal contact with three of the main objectors in an effort to clarify some the points raised and correct some misunderstandings. Their reaction, I thought, was understandable, since the first they knew about the proposed scheme was from a press report which gave the impression that their property was going to be taken from them. It must have been quite a shock at the time.

Although on our visits we got a hospitable welcome, we were left in no doubt about the strength of their opposition.

## Road Non-Sense

It was not just private landowners who were reluctant to co-operate. A much more immediate and serious difficulty was with the DOE Roads Service.

During my preparation for making a formal planning application for Phase One, I was aware that a key area of land between the car park and the track bed was occupied by DOE Roads Service and used by them as a materials storage depot. The compound was surrounded by a secure timber fence with double palisade gates which effectively cut us off from the car park, our only access to Ballydugan Road being via a narrow farm lane.

In an effort to improve our access, I approached the local Roads Service in Downpatrick in July 1984 to find out if they would be prepared to release some of this land for the railway project, in particular for our Workshop and Station Building. During our meeting it became clear that in fact, Roads Service did not have legal title to the land which they occupied and that it was still owned by Lord Dunleath. Needless to say, the meeting concluded without further discussion.

Elated, I left this meeting and walked down English Street to the offices of Alexander Reid & Frazer, Estate Agents acting on behalf of Dunleath Estates. After explaining the situation to Hugh Press and informing him of the enormous importance of this land to the railway project, the matter was drawn to the attention of Lord Dunleath. The result was that this area of ground subsequently became included in the railway lease for Phase One.

(The land referred to is now occupied by our Station, Workshop and Secure Compound)

I soon discovered that getting title to the land was one thing, but getting possession was quite a different matter. It was to take another four years of persuasion to get possession. Roads Service had to find an alternative site before they could move out. The delay caused by having 'sitting tenants' on our development site was becoming a major obstacle in getting the building contract started. At one stage it looked as though we were going to be forced to relocate our permanent workshop to the north, outside the compound. As this would have created numerous problems for us, especially for future development and access, it was therefore a suggestion to which I was strongly opposed.

Eventually, it was September 1988 and the years of procrastination by Roads Service had become a stubborn road block to progress. Roads Service produced a letter dated 1976 which indicated that they had an agreement at that time but that a formal transfer of the land in question had not been completed. They therefore informed DDC that they did not intend to vacate the site.

A compromise was put to Roads Service, whereby they should evacuate that part of the compound needed immediately for the first phase of the building contract, namely a workshop. This proposal was also rejected. We now sensed danger. If the contract was not started before the end of the financial year we would lose our grant aid for both workshop and station building.

I reported this situation to our Board of Directors at the end of September, and informed them that a meeting had been set up for 4 October 1988 in order to try to resolve the situation with all parties concerned.[9] The Board resolved that if the meeting failed to produce the required result, then Eddie McGrady MP and director, Bill Gillespie, would make private approaches at the highest level to try to resolve the matter.

The subsequent meeting ended in deadlock and it was time to bring out our 'big guns'. This minor dispute, therefore, went all the way up to the Minister for the Environment, Richard Needham.

Thankfully, sense prevailed and the DOE agreed to vacate a 20m wide strip of the compound, thus allowing us to construct our Workshop. It was also agreed that one year later, they would release the remainder, allowing the construction of the Station Building. This was a long and very frustrating saga but one which thankfully had a satisfactory ending.

## Concrete Progress

By the end of 1984, I had prepared the drawings required for outline planning permission for a workshop and station building, together with the documents necessary for Listed Building consent. This was necessary as the listed Gas Works Manager's house was to be taken down stone by stone and moved across the road to eventually become our station building. Outline planning permission was granted in January 1985; by coincidence the date was almost 35 years to the day since the last train pulled out of Downpatrick. This approval had the proviso that development could not commence until an alternative site had been found for the Department of Environment, Roads Service, works depot.

Phases Two and Three would be much more complicated because, apart from land acquisition problems, the route of the railway to Ardglass crossed public roads and, at that time, reinstatement would have required a Private Act of Parliament. This requirement no longer applies.

Once again, Lord Dunleath offered to sponsor a Private Members Bill through the House of Lords, which would have saved us £7,000 and much valuable time. Unfortunately, as usual, things were not quite as straightforward and the outcome was that when we wished to proceed with Phases 2 and 3, we would need to promote a Private Bill. In order for this to happen, Lord Dunleath would not be permitted to act as Agent and we would instead have to employ a Parliamentary Agent and pay the necessary fees involved – all very complicated and expensive but, thankfully, this problem was yet some years down the track.

However, a year after receiving the Council's full approval, and with planning approval now secure, Ballynahinch councillors again tried to get the Council to switch its support from the Downpatrick scheme to the BCDRMT's Ballynahinch scheme.

It seemed incredible that after all the discussions and detailed examination of the two projects, that some councillors would still try at this late stage, to overturn the Council's previous decision and ignore the advice of their own Director of Tourism.

The situation looked very serious, as the Ballynahinch councillors appeared to have considerable support within the Council and we were expecting a very close result. It was obvious that the vote would be based on political alignment. All the time and effort expended, together with the exceptional progress made since receiving the Council's full approval, was now at risk. This ominous cloud shook the confidence of even the most experienced professionals on our Board and cast doubt on the ability of DDC to deliver in the long term.

When put to a vote, nine councillors voted in favour of the Ballynahinch project but the proposal was defeated by ten votes against. Our scheme was saved by just one vote. It is difficult now to imagine what the consequences would have been if the outcome had been otherwise, a reasonable assumption being that there would be no working railway museum now in Down District.

## Organisation

It had become obvious at an early stage that the success of a project of this magnitude would depend to a large extent upon the quality of the organisation put in place to develop, organise, and operate the many and varied activities.

We were very fortunate, at an early stage in our development, to be joined by Robert Edwards, a founder member of the RPSI and who until this time had been Chairman of that organisation. With his wide experience of railway preservation and his background in banking, his agreement to take on Chairmanship of our fledgling organisation was instrumental in our early successes.

The early involvement of our solicitor, Ciaran McAteer, contributed greatly to the success of our company and his professional guidance is still much appreciated. In addition to his legal input, he also served as a very efficient Chairman between 1988 and 1991.

By 1984, David Trotter had become involved and, with his background as a Valuation Officer, his skills in land negotiation would make a valuable contribution to future developments.

By the beginning of 1985 the type of legal structure for our scheme had been finalised with the setting up of two separate bodies, a Company and a Society. Up to this point we had being operating under the name Downpatrick and Ardglass Railway Society.

The Company would be legally responsible for all aspects of the Working Railway Museum, an arrangement which would best protect the interests of the general membership.

At the time, the decision to have two separate organisations was considered to be the better arrangement, as it allowed for a quick decision-making process which would not require the approval of the general membership, a device particularly advantageous in the early years of our development. The downside was the perception which gradually crept in among the volunteers of a 'them and us' situation which led to membership problems and resentment between some volunteers and members of the Board of Directors, even though most of the Directors were also members of the Society.

## The Company

The Downpatrick & Ardglass Railway Company Limited

would be a company limited by guarantee and without a share capital in order to enable us to qualify for charitable status. Initially, members would be restricted to the existing members of the Committee who wished to purchase a share (£100). Future members would be by invitation only.

The Company was established in August 1985, when eight members[10] of the Committee purchased the necessary shares to enable the Company to be formed. These members formed the Board of Directors and were legally responsible for the whole scheme as well as the appointment of the Management Committee.

By the following year we were beginning to attract additional talent, in particular Michael Collins, who, apart from having a deep interest in all aspects of public transport, was a lecturer in Business Studies at the College of Business Studies, Belfast, as well as a skilled communicator. His immediate contribution at management level was timely, considerable and of particular help to me. Needless to say, it was not long before he was appointed to the Board of Directors to fill the role as Secretary and eventually took on the responsibility of Chairman, a position he currently holds.

Initially, DDC did not wish to be represented on our Board, although Bryan Coburn would attend as liaison officer for the Council's Recreation and Tourist Department. However, from 1994 onwards the Council was represented on our Board by two appointees. During the succeeding years we were very fortunate to have this representation and interest from councillors[11] an arrangement which was to

***Above:*** Ciaran McAteer and Mike Collins

transform our working relationship.

Our Management Committee was also strengthened by the presence of our Curatorial Advisor, Ms Lesley Simpson BA, Keeper of Collections in Down County Museum.

The Management Committee was the key to the efficient operation and development of the project and was made up from members drawn from both the Board and Society.

The post of the General Manager was fundamental to the successful implementation of the decisions of the Committee and was difficult to fill as it was so demanding. Having held this position myself from 1985 until 1990, I was well aware of the many difficulties the job brought. In fact, it had the characteristics of a full-time occupation.

The last GM was Edwin Gray who, in 1998, volunteered to fill this post in addition to his role as Operations Officer. Edwin had just resigned as Head of Music at a well known Belfast school and was confident he could cope with the demands of this new position. For the following four years he performed this onerous task with great energy and professionalism.

During the period 2000–02, we were also fortunate to have the organisational skills of Jonathan Condell who became Chairman of our Company for a period until his employer, Nortel, put greater demands on his services.

## The Society

After the formation of the Company, the Downpatrick Railway Society was formed to accommodate all members on the payment of the required subscription. It would be from the Society members that the volunteers would be draw for the restoration, maintenance and operation of the railway.

The Society would also be responsible for fund-raising, publicity schemes and generally helping to further the aims and objectives of the Company. The development of social aspects would also be an important activity. The Society's most notable achievement over the years has been the production of the excellent publications of *DRS News* and *Downrail*.

As already mentioned, this two-tier arrangement created increasing resentment during the following years, some members of the Society believing that they were 'outsiders' and cut off from important decision making, although fully involved as hard-working volunteers. As the years passed, efforts were made to improve the situation and much time was spent trying to convince the membership that we were all on the one team. In latter years Edwin Gray was partially successful in keeping things on an even keel for a while but the problems continued to simmer. Something had to be done.

It was not until 2004, after Edwin's and my own retirement from the Board, that steps were taken to provide a more democratic structure by the dissolution of the Society with all members joining the Company. The Board of Directors was abolished and all members were now eligible to vote for appointments to the Management Committee.

The other significant change at this time related to the name of the Company which was changed from the long established Downpatrick and Ardglass Railway Company Ltd to the Downpatrick and County Down Railway Society Ltd. Our trading name of Downpatrick Railway Museum was also abandoned.

One reason for changing the name of our organisation was that having Ardglass in the title was confusing visitors, some of whom were under the impression that they could go there by train. Indeed on one occasion a group of visitors arrived at the station and split up, one party heading for Ardglass by car while the remainder sought to obtain tickets to Ardglass!

These changes have certainly improved the general atmosphere, although there is nobody to blame now when things go wrong. Whilst it resolved one problem, it has created another because, with this new arrangement, there is now no place for the involvement of influential individuals, (not necessarily railway enthusiasts), who, in the past were prepared to devote some of their valuable time, business experience and influential contacts to assist in our development. The rapid progress of the first 20 years would not have been possible without this contribution.

***Right:*** Volunteers were not recruited quite as young as this! In March 1993, Wesley Johnston (now one of two MDs at Colourpoint) is photographed at the Loop Platform with a Downrail cap.
*Norman Johnston*

**Footnotes**

1 Action for Community Employment – Chapter 6.

2 *Down Recorder* 26/08/82.

3 *Down Recorder* 23/09/82.

4 Bryan Coburn, Gerry Cochrane, Bill Gillespie, Eddie McGrady, Bob Pue, Dr Brian Turner.

5 Bryan Coburn, Gerry Cochrane, Robert Edwards, Bill Gillespie, Eddie McGrady, Bob Pue, Dr Brian Turner.

6 Gerry Cochrane, Robert Edwards, Bill Gillespie, Ciaran McAteer.

7 Bob Beggs, Bryan Coburn, Gerry Cochrane, Robert Edwards, Bill Gillespie, Cyril Leathers, Ciaran McAteer, Dan McNeill, Peter Scott, Brian Quinn.

8 Gerry Cochrane, Robert Edwards, Bill Gillespie, Paddy Forde, Pat Magee, Brian Quinn.

9 Present- Messrs Frazer, Graham & Lewis (Roads) Cochrane (Railway Museum) Press (Alexander Reid & Frazer) O'Connor & Cunningham (DDC)

10 Gerry Cochrane, Robert Edwards, Paddy Forde, Bill Gillespie, Colin Holliday, Pat Magee Ciaran McAteer, Jim Perry.

11 Adams, W Alexander, P Craig, J McIlheron, P Toman, Mrs A Trainor.

# CHAPTER 3

# CHARIOTS OF DESIRE

By the summer of 1984 we realised that our scheme had the potential to succeed and, bearing in mind that the heritage of the local Edwardian railway was quickly disappearing, we would need to move fast in order to acquire a representative collection of artefacts of that period. This was a bit like putting the carriage before the horse, but it was most essential in this case. I was aware that vintage carriages, in particular, were of fundamental importance to the eventual success of our scheme.

There were two major problems with this strategy, the principle one being that at this early stage in our development, finance was in very short supply. To move a carriage body, usually between forty and fifty feet long (12m & 15m), would require the hire of at least one crane and a lorry for a day.

Secondly, we had no suitable safe storage accommodation. However, if we had decided to wait until these problems had been resolved, most of our unique collection would not exist to-day.

The vintage carriages described in this chapter are particularly relevant to our 'mission statement' (see Chapter 10), in having the potential for a unique and important collection.

## Royal Connection

1984 marked the start of a long and hectic period of carriage acquisition beginning with the BCDR Royal Saloon, an acquisition which was a once-in-a-lifetime opportunity and one which could not possibly be ignored.

This carriage was in a frightful condition with most of its external panelling and doors missing or hanging off as well as the floor in an advanced stage of collapse. Apart from these defects it was still structurally sound and, surprisingly, most of its original internal panelling, including some sepia photographs, had survived, although in poor condition. We

decided that it was definitely a candidate for preservation.

This magnificent carriage was built for the BCDR in 1897 by the Ashbury Railway Carriage & Iron Company of Manchester for the proposed visit of the Duke and Duchess of York in that year. With a length of 48ft (16.6m) it comprised a centre saloon with a small pantry and adjoining toilet, together with a ladies' saloon at one end and a gentlemen's' smoking room at the other. The most notable features were the glazed bow ends and clerestory roof. It was described by the press when first delivered as "the most wonderful carriage ever sent to Ireland"

It is incredible to think that this opulent carriage was designed, constructed and delivered within six months of the order having being placed.

During a test run to Downpatrick prior to the royal visit, the carriage made a dramatic entrance into the station when its roof vents collided with the platform canopy fascia to the accompanying sound of splintering wood. I am sure this event caused a few red faces, not to mention having to work overtime to repair the damage.

When not in use for royal visits, it was stored under cover at Queen's Quay, Belfast, headquarters of the BCDR. After many years of idleness, it was converted in 1923 into a first-class saloon; the only structural change made to it then was the provision of an additional door at each side and formal seating arrangements were introduced along the side walls.

During the remainder of its working life it was used principally by golfers on the 12 noon Saturday express to Newcastle. It became known as the Golfers' Saloon and the train as the 'Golfers' Express', the only named train on the BCDR.

After the closure of the railway this splendid carriage was purchased by a farmer from Hillsborough, County Down and for thirty-five years it became a sumptuous residence for chickens. So over this period accumulated chicken droppings had built up on the floor to a depth of 12 inches

*Above:* The interior of the Royal Saloon, as built.

(300mm). This mess had to be shovelled out and various loose bits and pieces of the carriage secured before it could be moved by road to its new location.

Although this was a tremendous 'find' the problem of safe storage was now uppermost in our minds and after weeks of searching for a solution, the RAF at Bishopscourt, County Down generously allowed us to store it on one of their disused runways. Although in the open and exposed to the elements, at least it was safe from vandals and, hopefully, from low flying aircraft.

Our problem of transport was solved generously by Walter Watson, steel stockist of Castlewellan, who kindly loaned one of his 50ft (15m) trailers for the big occasion while the traction unit and driver were generously supplied by the army. We still

*Above:* Royal Saloon at Bishopscourt. Tuesday evening squad: Colin Holliday, John Hughes and Noel Killen.

had to find the finance for the hire of two cranes, judged to be necessary because of the fragile nature of the carriage.

Heads turned in Downpatrick at the appearance of this once splendid carriage when it passed through the town on its way to Bishopscourt, ignominiously perched on the back of a lorry, now in a very sorry state almost 100 years after its first splendid visit in 1897.

Having been placed in a high security environment, volunteers who wished to work on this project all had to be subjected to a security check and we were all very relieved when these were issued to us in due course. Work commenced by providing protection from the elements as well as the installation of a new one inch

***Above:*** Arrival of the GNR 12 ton goods wagon.

(25mm) thick plywood floor. Most of the external panelling was also replaced during this period, with the exception of one end, which was left in its original condition, complete with all mouldings and fittings for future reference. The group on location at Bishopscourt became known as 'The Tuesday Evening Squad'.[1]

It was not until 1987 that the carriage returned to Downpatrick where it was placed on an under-frame in the safety of our new temporary shed to await restoration.

Ten years later, in 1997, I prepared and submitted a detailed application with costs for funding to the Heritage Lottery Fund for the full restoration of this exhibit to its former glory. Most of the work was to be carried out by our vintage carriage restoration team which, by this time had earned an enviable reputation.

By way of encouragement, Dr Billy Hastings, owner of the Slieve Donard Hotel in Newcastle, which was originally built by the BCDR in 1898, gave a handsome donation to assist with the restoration. Unfortunately, this application was turned down as a result of some financial difficulties we were experiencing with an ongoing HLF assisted project, the Maghera Goods Shed. However, they did not rule it out for future consideration and we hope for eventual success whenever we have suitable accommodation.

The next 'find', although of no great significance, was a goods wagon body donated to us by a farmer near Killough, in County Down. It was a GNR 12 ton covered wagon of

pre-First World War vintage but minus wheels and located in a field some distance from the road. This would have been typical of goods wagons entering Downpatrick on a daily basis and used for the transportation of cement and potatoes as well as general merchandise. An interesting feature of this exhibit was its internal graffiti, most of which referred to the Kaiser in less than flattering terms.

We were often encouraged by the kind offers of help from many local people in the area, sympathetic towards what we were trying to achieve. One such offer came from a local farmer and haulier, Danny Savage, whose services we were glad to avail of. Danny suggested using his tipping lorry to move the goods van for us. I had no idea that it would be placed on top of the lorry sides thus making the overall height very close to the maximum permitted and very precarious indeed, especially when the lorry rocked from side to side while crossing the uneven surface of the field, before reaching the road. As I followed this load to Downpatrick, I kept thinking it would end up festooned with a collection of telephone wires. So, as you can imagine, its safe arrival in Downpatrick was a big relief.

## Trains v trams

In the summer of 1985 we received a donation of another very historic, interesting and unique carriage body. This was a BCDR Railmotor, a great find as it was the only surviving

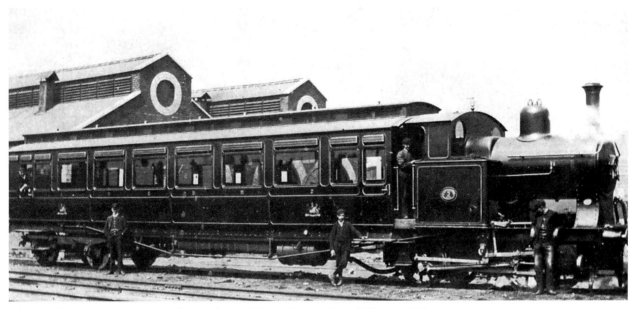

***Above:*** Belfast & County Down Railway railmotor No 2 at Queen's Quay Belfast in 1905.

example of the original three produced. When originally built in 1905 by the Metropolitan Railway Carriage & Wagon Company of Birmingham, the carriage had a small 0-4-0 Kitson steam locomotive permanently fitted to one end and a driver's compartment at the other. The advantage of this was that the train could be driven from either end and time was not wasted by having to reposition the engine after arrival at its destination. Its introduction was aimed at speeding up the train service between Belfast and Holywood, County Down, in a successful attempt at stopping the proposed competition from Belfast Corporation Tramways, who at the time was considering extending their tram service to Holywood. The Railmotors had their own platform in Queen's Quay and one can be seen in a Welsh collection photograph of 1914.[2]

In its original form it operated very successfully on the easy level track between Queen's Quay and Holywood, as well as the occasional run to Dundonald in the outer suburbs of East Belfast.

By 1918 however, these small locomotives were worn out, partly due to them being under-powered, and to poor servicing during the war. The solution was to remove the permanently fixed locomotive and replace it with a bogie so that the carriage could be used with a small tank locomotive in the conventional way, ie as a push-pull motor-train, while still retaining the driver's compartment and the benefits of the original configuration.

There were a number of advantages in having the locomotive detachable. For a start, it simplified servicing while also providing a quieter and more comfortable ride for passengers. It also allowed for additional carriages to be added.

## Disaster

This arrangement worked well during the next twenty-seven years, coming to an abrupt end in 1945 when a serious accident occurred near Ballymacarrett Junction in East Belfast, a short distance from the terminus at Queen's Quay. This accident occurred in the darkness of a foggy January morning. The motor train comprising a driving trailer and two six-wheel carriages was being propelled by a 2-4-2 tank locomotive when it crashed into the rear of a passenger train which had stopped for a signal at the junction. This was a very serious accident with many passengers killed or injured. Compensation claims were crippling for the BCDR which no doubt probably contributed to its rundown and closure five years later.

As a direct result of this accident the railway company discontinued the push-pull system and the original Railmotor carriages were used instead as conventional third class carriages, remaining in use until 1959.

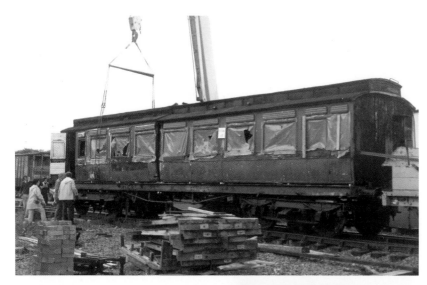

**Left:** The BCDR railmotor at Downpatrick, showing the two halves being joined on its new frame.

**Below:** The railmotor as we found it, seen from the driving end, with corrugated roof added.

**Opposite upper:** Queen Victoria's Saloon Carriage, London and North Western Railway.

**Opposite lower:** Ulster Railway Saloon carriage No 33 at Downpatrick.

During the twenty-five years preceding our acquisition, the Railmotor carriage had been used as a private dwelling, a welcome change from hens, and as a result, it was in reasonably good internal condition. The downside was that when purchased by the farmer it was cut in half to assist transportation by road to its new location near Gilford.

Some preparation was required before the move to Downpatrick, which included the removal of a corrugated iron roof and the demolition of a lean-to bedroom extension. In addition, because the carriage was in two halves each with an open end, each half had to be stabilised with cross bracing to prevent collapse during the journey. As well as that, a JCB had to be engaged in order to widen the entrance to the site beforehand.

All we had to worry about now on the home-ward journey was how to cope with the danger of bedroom furniture falling out onto the road. The scene was reminiscent of pictures taken during the war where bomb-damaged houses with beds, wardrobes and pictures on the walls were fully exposed to the world. In due course a suitable under-frame of the correct length was obtained and the carriage is now being restored by us to its former push-pull configuration.

Our first complete exhibit, ie one complete with wheels, was a three-plank open wagon, the recovery of which proved to be a long and unpleasant archaeological 'dig'. Looking back on this event I am amazed at the lengths we were prepared to go to in an effort to acquire some of these exhibits.

This wagon was unearthed in the dark and dirty Lisburn goods shed, buried and forgotten about by Northern Ireland Railways and probably their predecessors, the Ulster Transport Authority and perhaps even their predecessors, the GNR. Heaps of filthy rubbish which had built up over many decades had to be dug out manually to allow the wagon to be pushed out of the shed and lifted by crane. This operation took many evenings of hard labour but the opportunity to acquire a timber framed wagon in reasonable condition, complete with wheels, could not be missed.

I remember commenting grimly in the middle of one of these sessions, dripping with perspiration and covered in soot, that only railway enthusiasts would be mad enough to subject themselves to such punishment.

## Vintage Ulster

The year 1986 was becoming an eventful one with our most fascinating acquisition to date. This was obviously a first class saloon carriage, 25 feet (7m) in length, discovered near Gilford, County Down. The origin of this exhibit remained a mystery for many years but its design was intriguing. It consisted of two compartments separated by two toilets. Its most unusual feature however was its window design which in addition to having radius corners had heads and sills slightly concave. The only carriage resembling this that I have come across was Queen Victoria's Saloon, built for the London & North Western Railway.

Internally, the lower portions of the walls appeared to have been upholstered while the ceiling was painted and decorated with intricate lining. I felt we had a most unique example of a carriage of considerable age.

The discovery of this carriage was made by Kenneth Beattie, one of our long standing volunteers. Again, this carriage was on a farm although thankfully, in this case, it had been used as a children's' play house.

What a nice change this was. Unfortunately, sufficient care had not been taken with the foundations when originally installed, resulting in the base timbers becoming badly affected by wet rot.

Recovery was tricky, partly due to its poor base condition but also to the fact that it was wedged between a farm building and a very fragile pigeon loft. When swung by the crane, it missed the loft by inches, most of the pigeons taking flight in anticipation of a catastrophe.

A suitable underframe, originally a horse box with appropriate springing, was eventually acquired at Mullingar, County Westmeath.

Its origin was eventually solved by Mr Richards of Dublin as Ulster Railway carriage No 33, a First Class carriage with seating for twelve and built in 1862, rebuilt in 1890 and scrapped in 1920. It was last used by the GNR railway company in Portadown station as an office, before being sold.

## Into the Mountains of Mourne

No sooner had we got our breath back from all the excitement of the previous carriage when we became aware of another vintage carriage body which, once again, was the residence of hens, only this time situated deep in the Mountains of Mourne. This BCDR Second class six-wheel carriage, No 154, dating from 1918, was donated by Mr Frank McKinney of Dunmore, County Down. Although in reasonable structural condition it was situated in a field up a narrow lane with telephone wires adding to the difficulties of removal.

Arrangements had been made with Newcastle College of Further Education to accept it as an YTP project. Having

been to this establishment on other occasions, I was aware of the difficult access. After taking measurements I found that the side clearance into the building was only two inches (50mm).

On the morning of the move, a BT engineer arrived to disconnect the telephone wires. The crane arrived on time, as did Walter Watson's lorry with a 50ft (15m) trailer. Despite many efforts to get into the lane, the driver realised he was not going to make it and his only solution was to return to the yard and pick up a 40ft (12m) trailer instead. Meanwhile, the poor BT engineer was still up the pole, although in compensation he had a great view over the Mountains. The next attempt was more successful and the carriage was safely loaded and despatched on its way to Newcastle. It was a promising start but what was going to happen when we got to Newcastle? What if we couldn't get it into the building? I had no plan B.

At the Newcastle location, the idea was to carefully enter one end of the carriage into the workshop where rollers would be positioned under this end. The crane slings would then be repositioned to allow the carriage to be pushed further inside when additional rollers would be added. So with the carriage entirely supported on rollers, a final push

by the volunteers should complete the whole operation. Thankfully, on this occasion all went according to plan.

Work undertaken by the students consisted of re-panelling the exterior and adding new internal partitions, materials being supplied by our Society. Unfortunately, towards the end of its stay in the College all the original glass in the windows was broken. The feeling was that this was carried out by some disgruntled students, which sickened the staff so much that a decision was taken soon afterwards to return it to our custody, where it is still awaiting completion.

## Purchasing Fervour

The arrangements for the recovery of the above carriages were in the hands of David Trotter who proved to be a very effective organiser of such events. He had a unique ability to persuade people to donate almost anything in sight required for the advancement of the scheme. We all agreed that he had a brilliant 'brass neck' and this earned him the position on the Management Committee of Purchasing Officer.

In the spring of 1986, David, Colin Holliday and myself went off on a shopping spree to Mullingar and Inchicore in the south of Ireland and, before the end of the day, we

*Above:* BCDR Carriage No 154 entering Newcastle College of Further Education as a restoration project.

had purchased one Great Southern & Western Railway (GS&WR) bogie carriage No 836, two ballast wagons and one horse box (for use as the Ulster Railway carriage underframe). The ballast wagons were required as working exhibits which would be needed for future track-work.

During our search at Inchicore for carriages, I noticed that my two accomplices were taking an unhealthy interest in Maybach 'E' class diesel locomotives. They were all over these engines like ants. Inside, underneath, on top, their note books at the ready. I thought this rather strange behaviour for people from a steam railway, especially as no decision had been taken to acquire such locomotives. I pretended not to notice as I was well satisfied with our day's purchase. I was so pleased with what we had purchased that it reminded me of the occasion when I got my first Hornby train set.

Later in August we had to return south again to collect our 'train set' previously purchased from CIÉ, now Irish Rail. This was a two-day event to Mullingar where we would have to organise the loading of the two ballast wagons as well as a four-wheel underframe and a 50 foot (15m) GS&WR carriage. Judging from the number of volunteers who opted for the journey, it was a very popular outing. Either that or they were sent by the Management Committee to keep their eyes on what we were going to bring back.

The location in question was a marshalling cum scrap yard on the outskirts of Mullingar, situated beside the main Dublin line. This site was used exclusively by IR for scrapping redundant locomotives, carriages and wagons. One useful feature they possessed was a travelling overhead gantry crane which was going to assist us with the loading, although we were unsure of its ability to lift the body of the bogie carriage.

On the day of our arrival we couldn't resist the golden opportunity to gather as many spare parts from 'E' class diesels, carriages and wagons as time would permit. (In the interim we had decided to acquire two E class diesel locomotives). The parts we were most interested in included batteries, vacuum exhausters, starters, relays, vacuum bags and many other items too numerous to mention, which we thought would be useful in the future. Many of these smaller items were carefully stored inside the ballast wagons for transportation to Downpatrick.

Transport was arranged for an early start the following morning, so, having worked hard all day, it was back to the hotel for an early night.

Unfortunately, we were not early enough the following morning and by the time we arrived at the yard, loading had already started. The ballast wagons, the first to be loaded, were turned up-side-down for loading onto the lorries, the result being that now our 'goodies' were scattered over the yard.

The most nerve-racking operation was the loading of the carriage, which was to be lifted, we hoped, by the overhead gantry crane but without the advantage of spreaders, which we didn't have. Spreaders are essential to resist the inward pressure of the chains at roof level when under load. All I could find were some timber sleepers which we inserted on the inside to resist the crushing effect. Even with this precaution in place, the groans from the carriage during the lift were painful to listen to. To add to our stress the staff in the yard were anxious to quit, as the hour was now getting late. However, by the end of the day most of the items arrived safely in Downpatrick, the only exception being the carriage

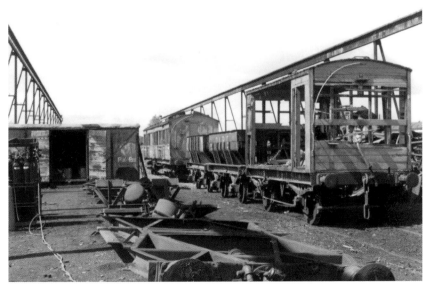

***Above:*** Horse Box (for undercarriage), two Ballast Wagons. and GS&WR Carriage 836

which arrived instead the following day, due to mechanical problems with the traction unit.

## Dublin-Cork Express

GS&WR carriage No 836, which, in its working life, operated on the Dublin to Cork route, might have seemed a doubtful candidate for our railway. However, it was of the correct period, having been built in 1897 by the Ashbury Railway Carriage & Iron Company, and at this stage in our development the opportunity to obtain a complete vintage carriage was not to be turned down. No 836 was a third-class carriage with the added bonus of being complete with its original under-frame and bogies.

Although we had no covered accommodation at this stage, repair work began in the open with the renewal of the bottom timber rails, 50% of which had been badly affected by wet rot. It was a very slow and tedious job, as all the vertical members were tenanted into this bottom member. In fact, serious restoration work did not begin until our new workshop was completed in 1990. This was our first vintage carriage restoration project and was completed in 1996 (further details in chapter 10).

## Fourth Class Travel

In the summer of 1987 we acquired a brake van as a possible short term solution to our need for a passenger vehicle. We felt confident that the track, as far as the Loop Platform, would be operational for Christmas and this would get our public operations started and thus secure some welcome income.

We had a choice of two at York Road Depot in Belfast, only one of which was fitted with a vacuum brake, thus making our selection easy. Vacuum brakes are essential on all passenger vehicles as it is the carriage brakes rather than the locomotive brakes which stop the train.

The van chosen was a 25 ton ex-LMS(NCC) one with an open platform at each end and a central compartment containing hand and vacuum brake controls. The plan we devised was to fit each platform with a guardrail and gates which would provide an external balcony at each end as well as some internal accommodation, not exactly first class, but certainly a step in the right direction.

The vehicle was delivered to Downpatrick in September and moved directly into the shed as a top priority project.

New roof covering, guard rails and painting were the main tasks to be completed before our first public train operation, scheduled to take place on 22 November 1987, The occasion was a visit by Officers and Councillors of Down District Council and Downpatrick Chamber of Trade.

The final major event of that year was the acquisition of a further unique vintage carriage, a six-wheel BCDR Brake Third, No 39, dating from 1903. It was an important acquisition in that it completed our BCDR vintage train collection and so would allow us the potential to fulfil our aim of operating a genuine BCDR Edwardian train.

For those readers who are not familiar with the different types of carriages required to make up a complete passenger train, a passenger-brake was similar to a standard carriage except for the addition of a guard's compartment with control of both a hand brake and the train vacuum brake. It also provided accommodation for passenger luggage and was marshalled at the end of the train. Its most distinguishing feature was the guards 'look-out', similar to a small bay window on each side of the carriage, which allowed the guard forward and rear vision.

This carriage was located in a field on the outskirts of Ballygowan, County Down and, fortunately in this case, had been well supported above ground level and was thus in reasonably good order despite having been used as a chicken house.

Recovery was going to be difficult, especially if the long grass in the field was wet, as access was across the field on a raising gradient, with a manoeuvre round the farm house and onto a narrow laneway.

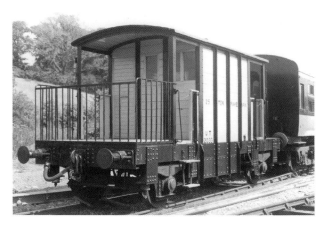

***Above:*** 25 ton LMS(NCC) brake van.

The move had been planned to take place during a dry period in order to allow a mobile crane and a 40 foot (12m) lorry access, while at the same time avoiding churning up the field or even worse, getting bogged down. However, as luck would have it, the night prior to the move saw heavy rain with the predictable consequences.

The lorry with the carriage on board promptly got stuck, the mobile crane which tried to assist got a puncture, and the farmer's tractor meanwhile was hitched onto the crane but made no difference. Thus, we had the tractor towing the crane and the crane towing the lorry and all going nowhere.

*Above:* BCDR Carriage No 39.

I had to charge around the locality to try and find additional pulling power. It was a Saturday and I was not hopeful. My imagination was running riot thinking of two abandoned vehicles left in the middle of the field. Again, I was asking myself "Why am I doing this?".

However, luck was in when I discovered a large four-wheel drive contractor's tractor belonging to Micwall Developments, but the only problem then was that Mr Walls, the owner, could not be located in order to approve the request for assistance. However, contact was made eventually and approval very kindly given. With engines revving, muck flying everywhere including over ourselves, we eventually succeeded in getting away from Ballygowan.

An unfortunate consequence was that when we had finished, the farmer's lovely green meadow looked more like Salisbury Plain after a session of tank manoeuvres.

Life was hectic during this period, with many things occurring at the same time. We were now faced with the need to consider acquiring four 'brown vans', BCDR No 148 carriage body, a 'G' class diesel locomotive, a signal box, a GNR bus (road vehicle) and additional track materials.

To make matters even more frenetic, this was all happening when I was fully involved in the preparation of sketch designs for the new permanent workshop and station building.

These were also difficult times financially, exacerbated by transportation costs throughout the preceding years. It became obvious that, with our limited resources, we had to be practical and selective. The 'brown vans' were definitely needed to provide underframes for the vintage carriage bodies and would also be used initially as mobile stores.

The BCDR bogie carriage had first and second class accommodation and would thus allow us to have the three classes represented in our vintage train.

The GNR road-bus was an attractive proposition which could have allowed expansion to our operations, but at that early stage in our development it was considered to be somewhat premature. It would also require covered accommodation for security purposes. Much to the disappointment of Michael Collins, a new member and a bus enthusiast, we had no option but to decline this offer.

## A Split Personality

BCDR Carriage No 148, referred to earlier, was definitely necessary in order to make up our vintage BCDR train and so was regarded as a priority acquisition. Again, it had been cut in half, when originally purchased by the farmer, to facilitate transportation to the farm for its intended use as a chicken house.

On inspection, my first impression was not favourable. The hens had not treated it with the respect it deserved. Nor had the farmer, who removed all the internal partitions which in time allowed the roof to sag and the walls to spread outwards at roof level. In addition, he had cut away a portion of the side-wall to form a large entrance. On further detailed examination, while superficially in awful condition, it was structurally reasonably sound and we were aware that it was the only one of its class in existence.

On arrival in our museum, because it looked so decrepit, the carriage was hidden in a remote part of our compound as a future, very long term restoration project. But as the saying goes 'the last shall be first,' and so it came to pass.

Considered to be in the worst condition of all our vintage carriages awaiting restoration, it suddenly became a candidate for the provision of necessary waiting accommodation at our future Inch Abbey terminus. The thinking behind this was that on an operating day this carriage would be taken out to Inch and parked in the bay-platform to provide shelter and other facilities for passengers.

I had considerable difficulty in persuading the Management Committee of the benefit of this proposal, which would in my opinion, have had three advantages.

(a) We would have a restored BCDR Carriage.

(b) Removal of an unsightly ruin.

(c) Provision of Period Accommodation.

The alternative was to acquire yet another 60 foot (18m) 'modern' carriage which would take up additional space on our restricted site and would further erode our Edwardian image. Fortunately, reason prevailed and we now have our first fully restored operational BCDR carriage.

It was not until the process of restoration began, that we realised that we had one half of carriage No 148 and half of No 152. Luckily both were of the same class. It was now a question as to which identity the restored carriage should assume. Carriage No 152 began life with the same internal arrangements as No 148, but later conversions reduced its accommodation by the addition of toilets.

It was decided that the original design with First and Second Class compartments without toilets was better suited to our needs; therefore the restored carriage would become No 148.

***Above and opposite:*** BCDR bogie carriage No 148 before restoration.

A period under-frame was acquired which was perfect in all respects except that it was two feet (600mm) too long. We turned this to our advantage by lengthening the body by the same amount, adding an additional door to provide double doors for disabled access.

A few years respite now followed until 1992, when GS&WR passenger brake[3] six-wheel carriage No 69 joined our vintage collection. This vehicle was complete and in reasonable condition although it had been built in 1888 and out of commission since 1968. It was purchased privately by one of our long standing volunteers, local dentist, Neil Hamilton, who is carrying out restoration at his own expense for eventual operation on our railway.

No 69 was a full brake (accommodation for only the guard and luggage) which would not be of much practical benefit, so Neil decided to retain the guard's existing accommodation in the centre and to convert both ends into fully glazed saloons. This would provide a very attractive observation carriage while still retaining the brake facilities

and therefore, in effect, having the best of both worlds.

Although our railway was to be primarily BCDR in character we were attracted by the idea of demonstrating other local railways, providing they were of the Edwardian period. This would allow visitors to compare the standards, design and comfort of different companies of the period. For instance, the BCDR was basically a commuter railway in comparison with the GS&WR which was inter-city and the design of the carriages reflect this difference.

The final addition to our vintage collection during the period covered by this book was a GNR third class, six-wheel carriage body, which arrived on site in 1993 and believed to be the only surviving example of its class.

## 'Modern' Chariots

Our Purchasing Officer's next proposal was to be the acquisition of 'modern' (1950s) carriages, which he reckoned would get train operations started while work progressed on the restoration of the vintage carriages. I felt obliged to remind David that his proposals would not improve the Edwardian image we were trying to create and would divert attention and finances away from the unique vintage carriage collection we were quickly acquiring, although I could see the merit in his proposal.

So now our immediate plan was the purchase of some operational carriages and so another visit to Dublin resulted in the purchase of three 61 foot (19m) long carriages. These were:

1  Brake Standard No 1918 (an open saloon with a guard's compartment).

2  Brake Standard Generating Car No 3223 (open saloon with a generator and steam boiler for lighting and steam heating)

3  Buffet Car No 2419.

All we had to consider now was the minor detail of getting them home to Downpatrick, by road.

The attempt to move them from Heuston Station in Dublin did not go according to plan. One problem after another was to frustrate our efforts.

The cranes had arrived on time and were preparing to lift the carriages off their bogies when the Chief Engineer sent a message to the effect that he would not release them. It seemed that he had not been informed that they had been sold to us. I instructed the crane operators to continue with their preparations hoping that the problem would be sorted in due course.

The next bit of news was that we would need a road permit from Dublin Corporation and so off I went in a frantic dash across Dublin to the appropriate department to plead for a permit. Apparently, it was not normal to issue permits on demand but, with some pleading, I eventually obtained one. On my return to Heuston, our transport had arrived, but lo and behold, it was a normal flat bed lorry and not a low-loader as was ordered. All the way from Lisburn near Belfast, the best part of one hundred miles with the wrong lorry.

The problem was that when the carriage was loaded onto the lorry it exceeded the overall height limit by about a foot (300mm). By this time it was obvious that the whole exercise was getting nowhere and would have to be abandoned. The cranes had to relocate the carriage onto its bogies and all the brake gear had to be reconnected. Perhaps this was just as well as I don't remember having got permission from the

Chief Engineer for their removal. Morale was at very low ebb. In fact one of our junior members was so disappointed that he cried all the way home on the train.

I should have been forewarned that our luck was running out, because on the previous visit to Heuston marshalling yard to inspect these carriages, I had parked my car well away from any obvious train activity in the yard. To my horror, when I returned to the yard after a brief meeting in the Station, one of our volunteers gave me the following message from the driver of the yard shunting locomotive. "I am very sorry for crashing into your car. I did not see it" I thought of what my poor long-suffering wife was going to say. Would she understand if I told her it was all 'in a good cause'?

Some weeks later a second attempt was made to move the carriages north. This time, a more sensible arrangement was devised of having them sent up by rail to Adelaide yard in Belfast. Strange that we didn't think of this in the first place. The first I knew that this event was to take place was when David phoned me at work to tell me that he had obtained two footplate passes for the following day to travel to Dundalk station, half way point between Belfast an Dublin to collect our carriages, which were at that time parked in a siding at the station. Our NIR locomotive was then to bring the three carriages up to Adelaide yard in Belfast. This sounded like a much more interesting arrangement than messing about with cranes and to travel on the footplate would be a first for me. Well, there had to be some perks for a General Manager.

All went well with this arrangement, although the journey from Dundalk proved very slow due to a speed restriction imposed on the train as a result of a suspected hot box (defective axle bearing) on one of our 'new' carriages. One big disappointment was that during the proceeding few weeks storage all the windows had been broken by vandals.

The final move from Adelaide to Downpatrick was scheduled for a Sunday at the beginning of May, when all three carriages would be moved as the special low loader we had hired was only available for one day. Each carriage would have to be loaded onto the low loader, the bogies onto a second lorry and the whole convoy comprising low loader, lorry, and two cranes set off for Downpatrick where the reverse procedure would be carried out. The convoy would then return to Adelaide for the second carriage and

***Above:*** Brake standard Generating Car No 3223.

so on until the third carriage was installed in Downpatrick. No mean feat.

By noon, with the second carriage now loaded, I was beginning to relax when the crane driver informed me that he was quitting for the day. I was furious and told him that the low-loader was only available for that day, a fact which failed to impress him. I phoned his boss and explained the situation and suggested that he should come and take over himself and fulfil his obligation. It is worth recalling that it was a beautiful summer's Sunday afternoon, ideal for the job in hand.

This idea did not appeal to him much and he asked to speak to his employee. We'll never know what he said, but it did the trick and the job was completed well before dark without any further hitches.

The forgoing events were the main activities during a very busy period for our active volunteers; paid staff would not have been able to match this.

**Footnotes**

1  Camac Clark, Gerry Cochrane, Colin Holliday, John Hughes, Noel Killen, Jim Perry.

2  *Railways in Ulster* by Grenfell Morton

# CHAPTER 4
# IRON HORSES

*Left:* No 421 being unloaded in Downpatrick.

I should state at the commencement of this chapter that, like the vast majority of our visitors, I have no sympathetic feelings towards diesels. In my opinion, they lack the magic and personality of steam locomotives but I do concede that they have their uses, particularly for operating work trains during the construction of the railway.

The first diesel which came up for consideration as a potential working exhibit was the Sligo Leitrim and Northern Counties Railway (SLNCR) Railcar B. In June 1985, our Chairman, Robert Edwards, Colin Holliday and myself while taking part on a RPSI rail tour inspected this vehicle at Limerick Junction. It was not a pretty sight, having been badly vandalised and rumoured to have some other serious faults so it was considered not suitable for our scheme.

That was the thinking then. Twenty years later, shortly after my retirement from the Board, it arrived at our museum and is now awaiting restoration.

## German influence

In 1986 our Board of Directors decided to purchase two Maybach 'E' class diesel locomotives Nos 421 and 432, the whole class having been taken out of service some years earlier.

These engines[1] were built by CIÉ at Inchicore in the early 1960s and were fitted with Maybach diesel engines rated at 400hp together with hydraulic transmissions, both units being manufactured in Germany. The Maybach engine was developed for the German navy in World War II for use in U-boats as well as powering the Panther and Tiger tanks. Its main feature was a tunnel crankcase and a 'disk-web' crankshaft with large diameter roller bearings, which gave the advantage of quieter running and ease of maintenance.

It was decided that locomotive No 421 would be restored to operational condition, while No 432 would be used as a source for spare parts.

The acquisition of locomotive No 421 was very generously sponsored by Bill Gillespie and to mark his generosity, the locomotive was named after him, *W. F. Gillespie OBE*.

However, making these purchases was the easy bit; getting them to Downpatrick was a daunting prospect but, with the offer of assistance from our friends in the RPSI and with the generous co-operation of WJ Law & Co, in providing the low loader at reasonable terms, by the beginning of November we were on the move.

Both of these locomotives were in store at Inchicore Works in Dublin where we began the preparations for the first move of locomotive No 421. We were very fortunate at the time to have with us Peter Scott from the RPSI who, with his long experience in dealing with such events, was a tremendous help.

In addition to giving his valuable time, he also arranged for the RPSI rail-ramp equipment to be made available and demonstrated to us the best method of setting it up. This ramp consisting of tapered rails, sleepers and packing and when assembled, was to connect the running rails with the tail of the low-loader lorry. This operation was carried out by our enthusiastic squad of volunteers[2] under Peter's supervision.

As we were about to begin the loading procedure, a CIÉ workman appeared with oxyacetylene gear, to cut off the buffers. I was certain that the overall length of the locomotive would not be a problem and informed him that his services were not required as I had already checked the measurements beforehand. Fingers were crossed, however.

Within a few hours we had the ramp assembled and began winching the locomotive up the ramp onto the low-loader. An hour later we were ready to depart.

The journey to Downpatrick through the streets of Dublin, with a police escort, was taken at a slow pace, but once out onto the open road, I was surprised that the convoy was able to do 50mph, and this was some time before the new motorway had been built.

The most tedious section of the journey was the delay at the Northern customs post, where red tape had us tied up for hours. We had to take our place in the queue behind a

convoy of lorries, an unpleasant regular feature of all such imports from the South at that time.

One serious thought which kept niggling away at me all day concerned the final part of the journey, when the lorry would make its way across the DOE car park at Downpatrick. I was not too sure if the tarmac surface would take the 45 ton load, as this car park had been constructed on a bog. I had an image of two deep furrows gouged out from one end of the car park to the other and couldn't even begin to think of the reaction of the owners, our friends in the DOE Roads Service.

The off-loading took place the following morning in Downpatrick, when the whole process with the ramp was reversed. I can still remember the great feeling of relief when the job was finally completed, especially without any accidents befalling any of our volunteers – not to mention not being faced with a huge repair bill from Roads Service.

We had to return to Inchichore at a later date for locomotive No 432, when the whole process would begin again, this time having some useful experience under our belts.

## Resuscitation

Within days of delivery, No 421 was soon tucked up in the engine shed and it wasn't long before David Trotter was inside the engine compartment trying to get the loco started. The locomotive contained 12 heavy duty batteries which had to be tested, checked and charged. Pat Magee, to our great relief, took over the responsibility for this problem and arranged for us to bring them to Newcastle College where, in correct laboratory conditions, students could carry out the proper procedures under his supervision. These locomotives had to be pre-heated for about two hours before they could be started and so were fitted with a 9kw immersion heater for this purpose.

After weeks of preliminary checking, the time arrived to go through the starting procedure. On the first occasion when the starter was engaged the six-cylinder Maybach engine turned over, produced a lot of acrid smoke, spluttered a few coughs, but alas, refused to come to life. By this time we were nearly all gassed and enveloped in thick fumes, but I can recall thinking that the production of smoke indicated some progress at least. The fact that it actually turned over was a pleasant surprise, as it had been out of service for years.

***Above:*** Early days with No 421, seen here in 1988.     *Drew Sucksmith*

Excitement was increasing and, after allowing time for the smoke to disperse and the batteries to be recharged, a second attempt was made. The starter whirled, the engine produced even more smoke and fumes, coughed once, more smoke, coughed twice, but still refused to respond. But the signs were promising and at the fourth attempt the engine sprang into life. Loud cheers ringing out from all spectators could be heard for miles around. The noise produced inside the corrugated iron shed was deafening, yet sounded like sweet music to our ears after all the waiting and effort involved. I had been filming the whole event through the smoke and darkness within the shed, producing a result depicting a scene from Dante's Inferno

There was a distinct feeling of pride among our volunteers and even I was pleased for what had been achieved so far. No attempt, of course, was made at this stage to engage the drive, as many tests and adjustments would still be necessary before any of that could be contemplated.

I can remember one incident in particular which occurred during these 'adjustments'. The engine was ticking over,

better described as roaring at full 400hp, while David and myself were inspecting a valve which was located outside the engine, near track level. David was on his hunkers cautiously opening and closing this valve but without any effect. I was standing behind ready to beat a hasty retreat. It appeared as if this valve was blocked so the obvious answer appeared to be to unblock it using a suitable piece of wire. Although this did the trick, the jet of compressed air sent us both flying head over heels across the workshop floor. It is a pity this dramatic scene hadn't been caught on camera.

After this incident, I considered that brake testing should prove interesting, particularly as our length of track was just about 50m and, therefore, we had to be certain that when we got the engine moving, it could be stopped when required.

Early one frosty morning towards the end of January 1987, the locomotive was once more successfully started in preparation for testing the various systems, including brakes.

We knew that the air pressure system was the key to

success because once the operating pressure was attained, then all other systems should 'click in'. The next few minutes had the potential to become an historic occasion, providing all went according to plan but, with so much excitement among the bystanders, it would have been understandable if the driver was to overlook the handbrake. However, I felt confident in David's skill as he had previously taken the trouble of gaining experience in driving one of these locomotives at Westrail, County Galway.

My main anxiety, however, was in his selection of the correct gear, which in this case should be reverse, as forward gear would have sent the engine through the shed wall, resulting in the collapse of the entire shed down on top of us all. As usual, my feverish imagination was again working overtime.

The big moment arrived, reverse gear selected, hopefully, accompanied by deafening noise. Thick smoke billowed out in the confines of the tin shed impairing our vision, making it difficult to see which way the locomotive was moving, if at all.

With relief, we soon saw that the engine was moving in the correct direction out of the shed and along the track, to the cheers of all the waiting onlookers. Would the brakes work at the end of the short length of track? Thankfully, they did and for the remainder of that day, David had the locomotive running up and down the track giving footplate rides, his excuse being that he was 'just testing'.

The historic nature of that day's event was not lost on us, as this occasion was the first time a locomotive had moved on rails in Downpatrick since the railway closed. I felt particularly pleased with all our achievements thus far.

Incidentally, we discovered some months after we had purchased these locomotives that No 421 had the worst reputation in the whole fleet and that, in the opinion of the Irish Rail drivers, No 432 was a much better engine.

One interesting anecdote is that early in its life[3], in September 1962, No 421's worst case of bad behaviour occurred. On this occasion the locomotive with a 'trial train' of old bogie coaches was approaching Newbridge near Dublin on a falling gradient at 60mph when it became derailed just after passing the station. It smashed into a bridge abutment, resulting

in disastrous consequences for the rake of carriages. As a result of this accident, a 25mph permanent speed limit was imposed on all members of the class.

# G class

With the experience now gained, the need for a simple diesel shunting locomotive, which did not require a two hour pre-heating sequence, was discussed at length on many occasions and an ex-CIÉ 'G' class locomotive appeared to be the answer. It was not until 1989, when our locomotive situation had reached a critical stage, that discussions with Westrail produced an agreement to lease G613.

This was a diesel–hydraulic locomotive built by the German firm Deutz in 1961 and fitted with a 190hp V8 engine with chain drive. Although these locomotives had a poor reputation on CIÉ, reputed to be from being overworked on unsuitable duties, No 613 was expected to be very useful to our railway for shunting and work trains.

This locomotive was eventually purchased by one of our Directors, the late Jim Magorrian, a local jeweller. This very generous gesture was much appreciated by all our members.

Eventually two further examples of this class of locomotive were to be acquired (G611 and 617) both on loan from the Irish Traction Group at Carrick-on-Suir, County Tipperary.

***Above:*** G613 with owner Jim Magorrian.

*Above:* G611 and G613 at the Loop Platform in November 1998. No 611 is on loan from the Irish Traction Group.

*Drew Sucksmith*

*Above:* RB3 outside the shed at Downpatrick.

*Above:* RB3 at the bay platform, Downpatrick, in October 2003. *Drew Sucksmith*

## What! Another diesel?

Yes, another diesel, although in this case I have no one else to blame but myself. In a moment of weakness, I suggested at a management meeting that the NIR Leyland Railbus, RB3[4], which was then currently on display in the UFTM, might be useful for off-peak operations. No sooner were the words out of my mouth, than our Company Secretary and fellow Director at that time, Mike Collins, was drafting a begging letter to NIR. Mike was a keen enthusiast of buses as well as locomotives, so what could be better than having a rail bus.

This exhibit would not exactly improve our Edwardian image but it was in very good condition and would be ideal for mid-week operations. Further advantages were that it had a cab at each end and most importantly, could be started from cold.

It was originally built in Derby in 1981 as one of four experimental vehicles by British Rail Engineering and British Leyland to operate on British Railways. It was purchased in 1982 by NIR, re-gauged to the Irish standard gauge for use on the Coleraine to Portrush branch. It was not popular with train crews, mainly due to the fact that it had only one door on each side. After a period on display in the UFTM it was on the move again, this time with a satisfactory lease having been negotiated, to a new home in Downpatrick.

Sadly however, its period in Downpatrick has been one of inconsistent and unreliable operation as it had a

*Above:* Interior view of the railbus in operation in 2007. *Norman johnston*

habit of stopping for no apparent reason and at the most inconvenient times. We believe these problems have now been resolved and the vehicle is regarded to be operational.

There was an amusing episode associated with the acquisition of the railbus. After the management committee had agreed to acquire it (the UFTM being agreeable to the plan), Bill Gillespie, who moves in exalted circles, was asked, if he got the opportunity, to put our request for the vehicle to Ted Hesketh, Chief Executive of Translink, the railbus's owners. Bill, who was not himself familiar with the vehicle, duly got the opportunity to speak to Ted and put to him our request. To his disappointment Bill reported back that Ted had refused the request, as Translink "still needed the buses".

This answer puzzled Mike Collins as he knew that there was only the one railbus in Translink's ownership. Shortly afterwards Mike met Ted at a function being held in the UFTM's railway gallery. Ted told Mike that he had been approached by Bill and repeated the statement that Translink still needed the 'buses'. Mike then pointed out that there was only one railbus in Translink's ownership and it was right behind Ted! Astonished, Ted turned round, looked at RB3 and said, "Is that what you're after? Oh, you can have **that**! I thought you wanted one of the rail-link buses!" These were the road buses that ran the shuttle service between Central station and Belfast city centre.

## Steam locomotives

From an early stage in the development of this project it was recognised that the main difficulty would be in sourcing suitable steam locomotives. Any local locomotives that survived into the 1980s were either already in various museums or secured by other interested organisations.

We would have to look beyond the island of Ireland, to the only other countries which also operated on the Irish track gauge, namely Brazil and South Australia.

My inquiries brought me into contact with the President of the Australian Railway Historical Society, who informed me that they had four operational locomotives with another one undergoing restoration. The remaining 50 to 60 were either in the Mile End Railway Museum or on static display in various parks throughout the state. In his opinion, they were all beyond economic restoration but in any case, he was not prepared to let any of them go.

He thought that the situation was similar in the State of Victoria where they had five or six operational locomotives, with additional ones in the process of, or awaiting, restoration.

The situation in Brazil was a different matter and our hopes were raised by events taking place there. We became aware, through the RPSI, of the possibility of obtaining two small 0-4-0 steam locomotives in operational condition

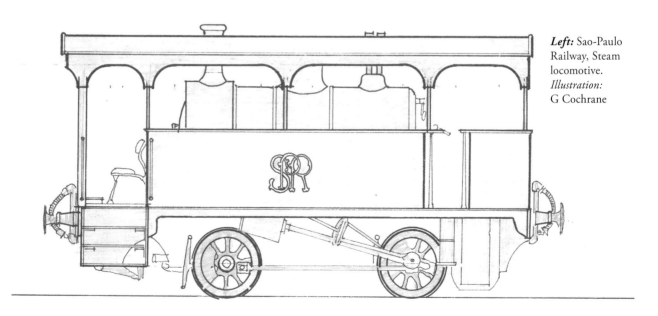

*Left:* Sao-Paulo Railway, Steam locomotive. *Illustration:* G Cochrane

from the Sao Paulo Railway.[5] The British Overseas Railway Historical Trust (BOHRT), together with the Associacao Brasileira de Preservacao Ferroviaria, were working together to identify the level of interest in preserving surplus steam locomotives. This situation arose as a result of the Brazilian Ministry of Transport's Preservation Programme which intended to establish a museum in the area.

Although these locomotives were not the most practical for use in our project, at least they were steam.

Of interest to us were two 0-4-0 tram engines, built by Kerr Stewart and Robert Stephenson in 1900 and 1902 respectively. At the time of our inquiry, in the autumn 1985, antique locomotives had a similar classification to antique motor cars in Brazil and could not be exported. An exception, however, was obtained in this case and both engines were offered to us.

What about the transport costs, you may well ask? At this early period in our development we had no funds and were barely able to cover postage costs. The prospect of obtaining the estimated $13,000 per engine was daunting. These costs were based on transportation to the Port of Santos, then Santos to Tilbury, by Furness Withy, and including cranage at both ports. It did not include the costs for the last stage, Tilbury to Downpatrick.

A second option was to ship with Houlder Ltd, which operated a monthly service to Waterford. This was expected to be considerably cheaper but still well beyond our financial ability.

An unexpected ray of hope developed through a contact in the Industrial Development Board, when a London businessman with an Irish background was hopeful of raising the funds necessary for the transportation costs of both engines.

On the strength of this, we wrote to the BORHT accepting the two locomotives. However, arrangements became rather protracted and were brought to a close eventually when we received the news that our sponsor had suffered some misfortune and would be unable to help.

Our failure to acquire these locomotives was a big disappointment at the time. On the plus side, however, the setback was to lead directly to a most unusual and productive relationship in an unexpected quarter as described in Chapter 8.

# My kingdom for a steam horse

The pressure was mounting on us to prove that we would be able to provide a suitable steam locomotive.

In desperation, we began negotiations with the UFTM for the loan of one of their small locomotives, with the proposal that the engine would be restored by the RPSI at Whitehead. For various reasons our approach to them failed to produce the required result.

Our next port of call was the RPSI itself, with a request for the loan of their 'Guinness' engine. These negotiations dragged on for a considerable time and the delay was beginning to affect progress on site, as the DDC's ACE scheme could not begin until we could produce a letter of intent regarding the provision of a steam locomotive.

**Above:** *Guinness* at the Loop platform in September 1989, prior to receiving its blue livery. *Drew Sucksmith*

Eventually, a formal agreement was obtained for the loan of the Guinness locomotive. So 1987 started on a high note with the arrival of this much sought after engine at our museum in Downpatrick.

This decision was a major milestone in the development of our project and led directly to the NITB giving a grant to assist with the restoration of the locomotive. It also allowed DDC to arrange an ACE scheme and to apply for an EU grant under the Special Cross Border Tourist Grant Scheme for the construction of a workshop and station building.

'Guinness' BG3 was an 0-4-0ST which had been ordered from Hudswell Clarke in 1919 for shunting wagons loaded with barrels of Guinness, from the brewery at St James's

Gate to the CIÉ main line at Kingsbridge in Dublin.

Because part of their route was through the city streets, the locomotives had to be classified as trams, designed with wheels and coupling rods covered with side plates in order to reduce danger to the public, as well as to prevent alarm to the horses then in use. These engines were also provided with a large brass bell to alert pedestrians to the approach of the train. When withdrawn from service, BG3 was presented to the RPSI in 1967 for preservation.

The original plan was for the restoration work to be carried out by our own volunteers, using the facilities at the RPSI workshops at Whitehead. It was later suggested that consideration should be given to the possibility of the work being carried out in Downpatrick under the supervision of Robert Edwards. There were a number of advantages to be gained from this arrangement. Firstly, it would avoid splitting our workforce and would create local interest. Secondly, it would allow more opportunities for our volunteers to work on the locomotive and thus reduce costly travelling expenses. This suggestion got a favourable response from Peter Scott and the move to Downpatrick was scheduled for Saturday 10 January 1987. It was decided to have the official signing of the lease at Whitehead on the same day, in order to maximise publicity for both societies.

Within a few days of its arrival, and with the assistance of Jim Perry and myself, our Chairman, Robert Edwards, got to work re-tubing the boiler as well as the repair of the water tank.

Robert patiently explained the process involved in the removal and replacing of 130 two-inch diameter steel tubes. I was horrified, and wondered what I had let myself in for, as it dawned on me that I was going to have to work inside the firebox! The procedure was first demonstrated by the redoubtable Robert, who had already prepared a steel drift (punch) for this task. Taking off his coat and arming himself with a sledge hammer, he proceeded to worm his way into the firebox. In order to understand the magnitude of this performance, I should explain that the firebox door is

***Above:*** Barry White recording maintenance records of the work he has carried out on the Guinness locomotive.

roughly 15 inches by 12 inches (380 x 300mm) and Robert was 6 foot 4 inches (1.9m) and built in proportion. I could not believe it possible when he disappeared inside. After seeing this, I had no excuse but to follow his example.

Inside, the firebox was dark and sooty with just sufficient room to stand upright and swing a sledge hammer. It was also a two-man job, one in the firebox swinging the sledge, the other in the smokebox, which is a section situated at the front of the locomotive just below the funnel. Whoever was in that position had to guide the tubes through the holes in the tubeplate. I was surprised to learn that the tubes were not welded but depended on a tight fit to make them steam tight. I was told that care was needed to prevent damage to the copper boilerplates through which the tubes passed. We took turns at this job although, to be truthful, Robert did most of the heavy work and it was a process which was to take many months of hard labour, although in our case, a labour of love.

With all the tubes removed and the two-inch diameter holes in the copper tube plates repaired, we made ready for the replacements.

I wondered what the procedure would be, but found that inserting the new tubes was more straightforward than I had anticipated, the only problem being in lining the tube up with the hole at the far end. When in place, both ends had to be expanded with the help of an expander, kindly loaned by the RPSI.

The next big job to tackle was the water tank. This was located on top of the boiler in the form of a saddle made of steel and about 12ft long. Its condition was not good, corrosion having created many holes and weak spots. In this case the tank should have been scrapped and a new one fabricated but this would have been costly and time consuming, so we used an alternative which was a combination of local patching and sheeting with fibreglass.

To allow this work to proceed we brought in a mobile crane on a Saturday morning to carry out the lift once all the pipe work had been disconnected and other obstructions removed.

As this work was in progress, all our volunteers downed tools and gathered around to watch the show.

The lift began slowly, and then stopped! We could

*Above: Guinness*, now fully repainted, approaches the Loop platform in 1990, with Down Cathedral just visible above the tree on the right.

not figure out the cause of the problem and, after much head scratching and time wasting, we found that a pipe underneath was still connected. I later discovered that one of our younger volunteers was aware of this but decided to keep the information to himself and enjoy the fun. We were not amused. This same individual was reprimanded for behavioural reasons relating to another incident and was eventually excluded from the Society.

Many weeks work were to pass in the repair of the water tank before it could be reconnected and the locomotive made ready for painting. Lots of holes were obvious even before removal and these had to be patched with steel plates welded into place. We were fortunate to have among our volunteers Richard Convery, a professional welder who made short work of this task.

If we thought that the visible parts were bad, we were in for a shock when we inspected the underside. Here, extensive corrosion had taken place to such an extent that patching was out of the question, leaving us with only one option – fibreglass. To carry out this task, the steel underside had to be scrupulously cleaned down to bare metal before layers of glass fibre and resin could be applied. Robert had given me very precise instructions on the procedure involved, which was to include the heating of the metal surfaces with oxyacetylene before applying the glass fibre.

The next stage was the painting, but before this could begin the locomotive had to go through many tests, adjustments and inspections over a period of months, before it could be passed as fully operational.

At this stage, Cyril Leathers took over, ably aided by Camac Clarke, and the long job of painting preparation work began. It was exciting to watch progress, each week being a week closer to completion. The final painting and lining took many patient hours of slow labour but the final outcome was magnificent. How splendid our first steam locomotive looked and how proud we all felt.

By 1989 the Guinness locomotive was finally completed and back in service, now finished in a livery of deep blue with white lining. This, together with polished brass nameplate and copper pipe work, was a truly magnificent sight and probably grander than when it entered the service of Arthur Guinness in Dublin in 1919.

## Continental steam

All the speculation and urgency regarding the need to acquire our own steam locomotives prompted the setting up of a group called the Irish Sugar Company Locomotive Group (ISCLG) to explore the ownership and possible acquisition of two Irish Sugar Company steam locomotives, stored for over ten years at Ballynahinch Junction.

After withdrawal from service in 1960, three of these locomotives were eventually purchased for preservation and moved by CIÉ to temporary storage at Dalkey Station, a few miles to the south of Dublin. Their protracted stay in Dalkey became an embarrassment to the railway company and one of the locomotives was sold for scrap to pay CIÉ's outstanding transport expenses in getting them there. The two remaining locomotives, Nos 1 and 3, were eventually purchased by an Englishman from Shrewsbury who planned to transport them to England.

However, shortly after purchase, the new owner discovered that he had a big problem, the substantial difference between the Irish track gauge and that of Great Britain. Consequently there was no point in shipping them across the Irish Sea.

***Above:*** The two Orenstein and Koppel locomotives, stored at Ballynahinch Junction in 1983.      *Norman Johnston*

In 1979 the BCDRMT arranged for the two locomotives to be stored at Ballynahinch Junction near Saintfield, County Down for possible use on their scheme. But as this scheme failed to progress, the two engines lay unprotected in a field for another ten years.

After extensive enquiries, it was discovered that the locomotives were still in the ownership of the Englishman and that he had received no deposit or other payment from the BCDRMT. When the ISCLG approached him, he confirmed that he was prepared to negotiate the sale of both engines.

***Above:*** O&K Locomotive No 3

A meeting of the ISCLG was hastily convened to discuss this matter, and the question arose as to who was free to go to England and complete the purchase. As luck would have it, my wife happened to be in Scotland on personal business at the time and during one of her frequent telephone calls home, I mooted the idea that I would travel to Scotland and meet her, the suggestion being that we could have a short holiday. This she readily agreed to, not being aware of my true intention. As you can imagine, she was rather taken aback when I told her of a slight change in our travel arrangements, but like the trooper she is, agreed to this slight diversion.

The journey from central Scotland to Shrewsbury was less straightforward than I had expected and resulted in the arrival at our destination after dark.

There wasn't a single light visible, giving an abandoned appearance to what appeared to be a former railway yard. Having sat in the car for some time, weighing up the situation and wondering what to do next, a door to one of the buildings opened and light escaped, helping us to establish which direction we should take. Fortunately, I had taken Robert's advice and written beforehand informing the

*Above:* O&K locomotive No 1, in March 1990, with cab and side tanks removed.

*Drew Sucksmith*

owner of my intended visit and of the possibility of a late arrival. The two brothers living within, later told me that they would have been away with their traction engine at a rally if I had not indicated our possible late arrival.

After a few polite preliminaries we got down to business, the contract was signed and the bank draft duly handed over. What a feeling of relief! I considered that in light of the generous spirit my poor wife had shown, the least I could do

*Left:* Locomotive No 3, fully restored, shunting No 1, which was in the early stages of restoration.

***Above:*** O&K locomotive No 3 in service, heading back from Inch Abbey on 16 April 2006 (Easter Monday).

*Wilson Adams*

was treat her to a meal in a local inn, but not before making a quick call to our Purchasing Officer to confirm our transaction and suggesting that he now made arrangements for the collection of 'our' locomotives.

By the time I returned from England, the two engines were safely installed in our museum, the only mishap being a slight 'rearrangement' of the farmer's entrance gates, which I understand was quickly put right by Robert with the aid of his JCB.

These locomotives have an interesting history, beginning in Berlin in 1934 with the construction of a batch of nine by the German firm of Orenstein and Koppel for the Irish Sugar Company. They were intended for the sugar factories at Carlow, Mallow and Thurles, each to receive three and were paid for by the Irish Government by barter with cattle, because of the unstable currency situation at that time in Germany. This was a few years before the outbreak of World War Two. It has just occurred to me that I have something

in common with one of these locomotives - we share the same birthday!

They were designed initially to shunt sugar beet wagons from the main line to and from the factories.

After 25 years of faithful service the sugar company decided that a more efficient system of propulsion would be desirable and in 1960 the steam locomotives were withdrawn and replace with G-class diesel locomotives leased from CIÉ. In recent years with the rail connection to the beet factories discontinued, the diesels also became surplus to requirements and three of the class are now in our museum. More recently, sugar beet production has ceased altogether and the factories themselves have been consigned to history.

## Heavy Lift

Every serious preserved steam railway should have a steam crane, as they played such an essential part in railway engineering and operations. They were usually parked in a siding and rarely seen by the railway traveller.

The first reference to what would become our crane occurred during a visit to our railway by NIR's Chief Executive, Mr Roy Beattie many years ago. During his tour I asked him about the possibility of NIR's ex-NCC steam crane, at that time stored at York Road, coming to our museum if it was surplus to their requirements. His encouraging reply was that if we could raise £500,000 for its replacement with a modern diesel crane, he might give favourable consideration to the request. Needless to say, the idea was quickly forgotten.

Years later, in 1994, we were surprised to learn that NIR had finally decided to scrap this crane and that it was now being offered to us at scrap value.

Built in 1931, by Cowan's Sheldon and Co[6], the crane consisted of three units: the main unit on two six wheel bogies with jib and boiler, a four-wheel water truck and a four-wheel match wagon. The total weight is in excess of 95 tons, it is 77 feet (23.5m) in length and had a maximum lifting capacity of 36 tons.

It was originally purchased by the LMS NCC railway to assist with the construction of the Bleach Green viaduct on the Larne line, some four miles north of Belfast As with most cranes, during its active life it experienced many dramatic moments, the first of which could have been most spectacular and which occurred during the construction of the viaduct. Perched high on the embankment at the end of the track with a twenty foot drop at the bridge abutment,

the crane began to roll towards the gap and was within a few feet of catastrophe when a member of the crew managed to apply the brake.

In November 1974, in a tragic event at Ballycarry near Magheramorne, while attempting to lift a loaded ballast wagon, the crane toppled off the embankment into a ditch, tragically killing one of the crew and injuring others. This particular event came close to ending the crane's life as well.

After withdrawal from service, it was moved to Larne Harbour station where it lay for some years, during which time our Board of Directors considered the offer and its financial implications. The cost of the move by road from Larne to Downpatrick would be the main consideration, estimated to be at £2,000, based on very favourable terms for heavy low loaders from W J Law & Co. Indeed, if it hadn't been for our friend Bertie Law, the eventual cost would have been much in excess due to the eventual problems experienced in the move.

Serious consideration by the Directors was given to the possible acquisition of this exhibit but the general view reached was that, although it would be a valuable addition to our museum, the

*Above:* The NIR steam crane after delivery to Downpatrick.

*Left:* The crane on display in 2004.
*Norman Johnston*

transportation costs were beyond our financial capability. Nevertheless, the thought of this impressive piece of railway engineering being cut up for scrap was just too much for one of our Directors, Jonathan Condell, who came to the rescue and generously offered a loan, (later converted to a donation), towards transport costs. This allowed us to take the decision to accept NIR's offer.

It took some courage for our Infrastructure Officer, Jim Carson, to volunteer to supervise the move[7], an operation fraught with difficulties. The move was frustrated by a number of unforeseen problems, the main one being unexpected delays occurring as a result of the inability of the low-loader to manoeuvre in reverse. The next problem was that the height of the load when mounted on the low loader exceeded the limit for the M2 motorway by two inches. To solve this problem, there was a delay of four days while an alternative route was cleared with the DOE.

Having taken care of all these headaches, the load eventually left Larne Harbour accompanied by a police escort, arriving in Downpatrick just before midnight. It was then that the real work began, first with having to construct a rail ramp from the low loader to the permanent track in order to allow the crane to, hopefully, roll off of its own accord. After working throughout the night it was mid-morning before the job was completed, an excellent

***Above:*** Ballycarry, November 1974. NIR has borrowed the CIÉ crane which is lifting the offending ballast wagon. In the background is the over-turned NIR crane, with broken jib.                                    *TN Topley*

demonstration of the enthusiasm and determination of most of our active volunteers and their sheer willingness to succeed.

It should be recorded, however, that while this was a momentous achievement for our railway, it could have resulted in some serious domestic consequences. We were unaware that some of our volunteers' wives had to enlist the help of the police during the night to find the whereabouts of their absent husbands!

### Footnotes

1   *Downrail* Nos 3 and 4.

2   Gerry Cochrane, Mike Collins, Robert Edwards, John Hughes, Noel Killen, Peter Scott, David Trotter

3   *Downrail* No 4

4   *DRS News* No 34

5   *Modern Tramway*, July 1987

6   *Downrail* No 9

7   *DRS News* No 20

***Above:*** John Reilly, Cyril Leathers and Edwin Gray on the steam crane.

## CHAPTER 5
# MAKING TRACKS

We now return to 1984 to follow the story of the track-laying.

In October of that year, a small band of volunteers[1] began working on site, clearing the Loop Platform and the adjoining track bed, a task which was to keep us busy for many weeks. When some of the undergrowth had been cleared, we were surprised to discover that the old platform had originally been surfaced with cinders and still retained the original pre-cast concrete edging. The main retaining walls along the platform face had originally been built with sandstone of which about 25% had been removed, taken for the construction of local fireplaces, no doubt, so leaving long stretches of the platform edge unsupported. The repair of this was a long and tedious job, with work mainly carried out by Noel Killen, one of our original volunteers and local building contractor who had a special interest in the conservation of historic buildings.

At this stage in our development our activities were confined to jobs which were not dependant on finance, as it was important to get volunteers started on various projects which would build up teamwork and develop enthusiasm, as well as inculcating new skills. Thankfully, the impressive, original wrought iron canopy still remained, although by this time its columns were seriously corroded. We also found that the entire original timber fascia boarding, with the exception of one board, had disappeared. It was obvious that this structure would require some serious restoration work. (See Chapter 6).

The track bed adjoining both sides of the platform was in a particularly bad state and, after 35 years without maintenance, had an accumulation of muck covering it to a depth of 12 inches (300mm). We were fortunate that Noel, with the use of his JCB, was prepared to spend many Saturdays clearing hundreds of tons of muck and vegetation in order to leave the track bed ready for track laying.

With the Loop Platform and adjoining track bed finally cleared, attention switched to the preparation for the future painting of the steel girder bridge, No 164. This was a rather precarious job, due to the fact that we were working on open girders above a very dirty river. Many hours were spent with wire brushes and chipping hammers to remove the accumulated rust and debris which had built up since 1939, the last time the bridge had been painted (according to a maintenance note still visible on the bridge). This project also included building brick retaining walls at each end of the bridge in order to retain the ballast. We were very grateful to Tyrone Brick for the donation of the necessary bricks for this task.

***Above:*** (Standing) Graham Leathers, Cyril Leathers, Robert Edwards, David Trotter, Noel Killen, Jim Perry, the late Hugo Smyth, Feargal Cochrane, and Niall Cochrane. (Sitting) John Hughes and Paul Killen.

# Yard Crane

In the spring of 1985 Mr Frank Trainor, owner of the former railway station at Castlewellan, County Down, offered us a yard crane which he thought might be of interest. This was a six-ton hand operated crane typical of those found at all of the larger stations on the BCDR, although Castlewellan was a GNR station. The crane was complete except for the jib, which had earlier been lifted off, although we were assured that it was "somewhere nearby".

I confirmed that we would indeed be interested and made arrangements to move it to Downpatrick. Little did I realise the difficulty which would result from that decision. I was not aware that this substantial piece of equipment was like an iceberg – two-thirds of it was underground!

The jib of the crane had been mounted on a central steel 'pin' about the diameter of a telephone pole, which extended about six feet (1.8m) below ground level and was set in concrete. In addition, an iron casting with five arms was located at ground level, the tip of each arm bolted with two-inch (50mm) diameter bolts bedded deep into the concrete foundation.

*Above:* The crane base.

Our recovery team, consisting of Cyril Leathers, my son Niall and I, naively set about the task with a jack hammer but after a few hours work we realised that we had a more formidable task on our hands.

The next attack we made was with a JCB fitted with a rock hammer, but we were a little restricted by a double-decker bus which had just arrived from Dublin and was parked too close to the work site. I was about to suggest to the JCB driver that perhaps we should ask that the bus

be moved and was surprised when he proceeded to put his bucket against the front of the bus, pushing it several yards out of the way, breaking the windscreen and putting a huge dent in the front. I should have mentioned that the scene of our operations was a bus scrap-yard!

After a couple of days spent with the rock hammer, the base was freed and the jib located under a mountain of scrapped buses Fortunately, little damage was evident apart from two iron tie-rods which were now bent. Once again, Danny's lorry came to the rescue and the whole crane was finally transported to Downpatrick, where the reverse procedure was put into operation for its re-installation.

*Above:* The yard crane.

This crane was to be positioned just outside our temporary locomotive shed, so accuracy in location was of the utmost importance in order to avoid obstructing any future track alignment, or worse still, having to move it again at some future date.

Great care was therefore taken in preparing the foundations, as we were expecting this crane to do some serious work in the future. Consequently, the foundations were on a similar scale to the original and once more the crane was very securely set for a further 100 years – or so we thought. But nothing can be taken for granted in our line of business and later it had to be moved again in preparation for a proposed new Carriage Gallery.

Its final position is in front of our new locomotive shed, awaiting full restoration.

# ACE Scheme

In January 1986, four full-time ACE workers began work to assist the volunteers in the task which lay ahead. This event marked the beginning of a period of incredible progress covering a wide range of activities. The arrival of these full-time workers on site had a tremendous psychological impact upon all the volunteers, who felt they were no longer on their own in this mammoth undertaking.

The first task for these workers was the diversion of a farm access road, in order to provide space for the erection of our temporary locomotive shed. This was later followed by the installation of a new security fence and gates, thus providing us with a secure compound.

Down DC equipped us with a 20ft (6m) container and a small wooden hut to help serve as a shelter, and to store tools and materials. Although conditions were pretty grim, (we had no heating or toilet facilities, the nearest toilets being public facilities in Market Street), we considered the absence of such home comforts could be tolerated for 'the greater good'. We still do not have heating in our workshop as the building is not insulated and heating would be inappropriate and expensive to operate.

## Basic Accommodation

During my earliest discussions with DDC's Director of Tourism, Bryan Coburn, I stressed the urgent need for a locomotive shed to allow us to store and carry out restoration work and to provide security for any locomotives or carriages which we would need, in order to get the project off the ground.

It should be appreciated that at this stage we had nothing to show to sceptical councillors or other funders that this was indeed a serious proposition. All I could offer in any discussions were promises. Although Bryan was enthusiastic and could see the potential, he had to persuade the Council that the investment was reasonable. Bearing this in mind, his initial approach was cautious to minimise the risk of a refusal.

His approach was that the cheapest possible type of shed should be considered, along the lines of an agricultural barn, to be used as a temporary building until such times as the Council could assess our seriousness and support.

This was not exactly what I had in mind,

but I could not argue with his logic and so obtained planning approval for a temporary shed.

The construction of this shed was assisted by YTP students from Newcastle College of Further Education's Building Department who built the nine-inch concrete block perimeter walls as part of their course – training to become bricklayers.

The budget was so tight that the concrete floor and inspection pits had to be constructed by our volunteers, who by this time were prepared to tackle anything which might help.

As temporary planning approval is limited to five years we had to make a new application after this period for permanent approval, which was duly granted. It is interesting to note that this 'temporary' building is still in use today, twenty years later.

## Track Laying

As soon as the temporary locomotive shed was completed, work began on laying the track. This was indeed a new experience for all of us[2] and at the beginning we felt we were taking on an impossible task. We really were like the early pioneers, having no lifting gear or proper tools for the various tasks. The exceedingly heavy components had to be moved or lifted using primitive techniques similar to those used in the building of the Egyptian pyramids; that is, with crowbars and rollers.

Some volunteers were asking how we were going to bend

*Above:* L-R, Noel Killen, David Trotter, Cyril Leathers, Desmond Bannon, Mike Collins and John Hughes.

*Above:* Michael Collins and David Trotter at work on the track into the new shed in late 1984. *Drew Sucksmith*

*Above:* David Trotter, lorry driver, Alan Major and John Hughes.

the rails for the curved sections of track. The question amused me as the query should have been, "How were we going to keep the rails from bending?", as 60-foot long rails are extremely flexible.

We got the first few lengths of track, including a turnout (normally known as a point) laid, using these primitive methods, before muttered protests could be heard among some of the older volunteers who were of the opinion that a 20th century JCB might be worth thinking about. Of course, once again, funding was the main obstacle. In this case however, we were once again most fortunate, as John Carson, Managing Director of HJ O'Boyle, the main building contractor in the town, was prepared to loan us

his machine and driver if available on Saturdays. This was a great asset and prevented a potential 'down tools' from some of the exhausted workers. It made a tremendous difference to progress and before long we were approaching the first bridge on the way to our initial goal, the Loop Platform.

It was now becoming obvious to us all, that mechanical aid, such as a locomotive, would be invaluable in assisting with our efforts to lay track. Up to this stage we had built a plate-layer's trolley to assist with moving tools, timber sleepers and other gear, but this had to be pushed manually along the track. As the track got further away from the depot, some of our older volunteers were having some difficulty and while not complaining, we were worried about them maybe expiring prematurely.

It was about this time, in early 1987, that our Maybach diesel locomotive became operational. I soon took back all I had said about diesels. With 400hp behind us, our track laying activities were to be transformed, particularly in regard to the handling and positioning of the 60-foot (18m) rails. Our simple but effective method was to tow the rail to the rail-head, disconnect and then re-attach the rail to the front of the locomotive and push it the last 60 feet over the sleepers. The only problem was that this locomotive had a two hour preheat requirement before it could be started. Some people are never satisfied!

By April 1987 our permanent-way gang had increased in numbers to include some new volunteers.[3] Morale was very high as great progress could now be seen.

*Above:* Works train leaving Downpatrick on restored track 1989.

***Above:*** The ballast train.

In September, rails, timber sleepers, and all fittings sufficient to reach the Loop Platform, had been delivered. Five strong ACE workers had made sterling progress with the reinstatement of the original railway fencing and were now employed during the week setting out sleepers, in preparation for the volunteers to lay the rails the following Saturdays. By October we had reached our first goal, the Loop Platform.

After the Christmas break the heavy slog of track work re-commenced with very slow progress being made due to bad weather conditions in the early months of 1988 and a delay in obtaining a turnout for the west end of the Loop Platform.

By this time Albert Sage had taken over responsibility for Permanent Way and, with his new, young enthusiastic team, was making great progress. By the end of the year the track had been laid on the main line side of the platform enabling the Loop Platform to be used as it had in its heyday with trains arriving on both sides. From this point onwards the Loop Platform became the centre of attraction for all public events.

## Enterprise Ulster

About two years later, the Council's decision to end the ACE scheme came as a very big disappointment to us all, particularly as this type of assistance had been factored into our scheme since its inception. However, the decision was forced on the Council by the Trade Unions, who raised objections to work being carried out by this form of labour.

After discussing the situation with Bryan Coburn (DDC) and reminding him of the importance of this form

of assistance to the future of our scheme, he came up with a new suggestion in the shape of Enterprise Ulster (EU), an organisation similar to ACE but better structured to suit our needs. This gave us new hope that all was not completely lost.

Three months after the demise of the ACE scheme, an EU squad consisting of a foreman ganger and four labourers took over from where the ACE workers had left off.

From my point of view, this was a much better arrangement, as proper supervision could now be provided.

Their jobs included fencing, setting out sleepers, rendering the shed walls and providing a concrete surface to the Loop Platform, as well as building a temporary platform with two sets of boarding steps to facilitate passengers.

Unfortunately, the EU scheme was also a short-term one and was replaced by a direct annual grant which allowed us to employ three full-time staff.

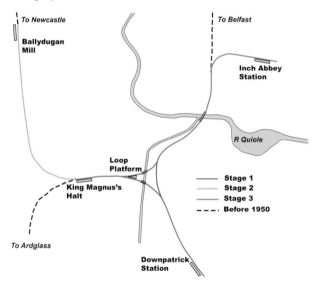

## Major Development

After the completion of the station building and workshop in 1990, as detailed in chapter six, consultants were appointed to prepare a feasibility study with costs, for the following major works which, due to uncertainties regarding land acquisition, would be divided into three stages as illustrated above:

**Stage One:**   Restoration of Loop Platform; track extension to west boundary; platform at Magnus's Grave; Loop line, including bridge

163; track extension to Quoile River.

**Stage Two**: Track extension to Ballydugan Mill

**Stage Three**: Track extension to Inch Abbey, including Quoile bridge, platform and restoration of gate lodge.

Having obtained the necessary planning approvals, and with grants totalling £398,800[4] agreed, preparations could begin without further delay. The completion of this work would have a profound effect on the nature and scale of our project.

# Stage One

During the first few years of our public operations, my concern had been mounting about the structural stability of the Loop Platform canopy. This wrought-iron structure had been built in 1892 and by this time, having been neglected for the previous forty years, was suffering from extreme corrosion.

The lower sections of the columns at their base connections had been reduced by corrosion to about 50%. Also, some of the iron roof trusses were so badly decayed as to be beyond restoration. Considering the exposed nature of the site, as an architect, I considered there was a risk of collapse and invited our structural consultants to provide a report on the general safety of the structure. The report confirmed my worst fears as well as providing a disappointing estimate of repairs, which would amount to £40,000. My report to the Board resulted in a decision to dismantle the structure leaving only the columns and scroll work, a very difficult decision as this structure was of great historical importance and a very valuable facility in our public operations. However, the safety issue was paramount and action was needed.

This decision came as a great shock to most of our volunteers and a rescue plan was proposed by the Society for restoration rather than demolition. Queen's University tested a sample of the ironwork and confirmed that it was wrought iron and therefore could not be satisfactorily welded. This meant that corroded components could not be repaired and would need to be replaced in their entirety.

The determination of the volunteers persuaded the railway's Board to allow them to try their ideas for saving the canopy. This of course greatly increased the workload but the enthusiasm of our already stretched volunteers knew no bounds and they commenced work with determination. As the work was expected to take years to complete, we had no option but to declare the Loop Platform out of bounds for public events when gales were forecast. In desperation we approached DDC for their help, pointing out the safety considerations but they refused on the grounds that they had no spare funds available.

It was a matter of great relief therefore that the International Fund for Ireland (IFI) were persuaded[4] to include the restoration of the Loop Platform in the grant package for the next phase of our development, as the repairs being carried to by our volunteers were proving more difficult and time consuming than anticipated.

In January 1993 work began on rebuilding the Loop Platform canopy. This involved dismantling the existing structure and saving the scroll work and cast iron stanchion base shells for reuse in the new structure. The only other component worth saving was the one remaining original fascia board. This was important as it would provide us with an authentic pattern for the replacement boards.

The new structure differed in two important details from the original. The first was that the original Georgian wired patent glazing roof lights were replaced with unbreakable fibre glass and the other was that all the steelwork, including the original scrollwork, would be galvanized. This would greatly reduce maintenance time for future generations of volunteers.

***Above:*** Loop canopy reconstruction

***Above:*** Track gang beyond the Loop: John McCutcheon, David Crone, John Reilly, Neil Hamilton, Walter Burke, Edward Duly, Des Sage and David Trotter.

The completion of the Loop canopy was another important milestone in the development of our working railway museum and one that restored an historic part of the BCDR. It was therefore fitting to have our opening ceremony on the platform where all our guests and volunteers could assemble and convey our thanks to Mr William McCarter, Chairman of the IFI, without whose generous grant, the development would not have been possible.

## Westward Ho

In the period since the closure of the railway, the track bed from the Loop to the Ballydugan Road had been used by the local farmer for gaining access to the lands adjoining the railway and it was a requirement of our lease that alternative access be provided. Therefore, before a contractor could be appointed for the track extension to our west boundary, certain accommodation works would be necessary to allow access to continue undisturbed. This work was to be carried out by our volunteers.

This entailed providing an access road adjoining the track bed between these two points, a distance of approximately 800 yards (728m). This was to be a considerable undertaking as it was necessary to keep the road at the same level as the track bed, (one metre above existing ground level, to be above flood level). It required an enormous amount of fill, approximately 2500 cubic yards (1,910m$^3$), which would have been very costly if obtained from a quarry, but we were fortunate in being able to arrange a free supply from a demolition contract which happened to be taking place in Downpatrick at that time. An additional further expensive item was the need for a bridge over one of the many drainage channels in the area.

With the accommodation works now carried out, the contract began for the completion of Stage One. The plan was that the track bed would be ballasted and left ready for volunteers to lay the track.

During this contract it became apparent that the completion of the project beyond our western boundary to Ballydugan (Stage 2) was going to be seriously delayed due to land acquisition difficulties, so it was then considered prudent to install the foundations for a temporary run–around loop at our boundary in order to allow trains in the interim to operate to this point.

The track in the direction of our western boundary would pass close to the historic burial ground of the Viking King Magnus, killed in 1102 and reputed to be buried with his men in nearby earth works. Therefore, we considered that a platform as this point would be justified in order to enable the public and in particular, visitors from Norway, to come and visit this historic site.

With the contractor's work now completed and the track bed ready to receive the sleepers, it was up to the volunteers to take over the track laying operation, a painfully slow process due to the considerable weight of the concrete sleepers and 60 foot rails. This was exacerbated by the fact that the site was inaccessible for our JCB so it was back to primitive methods, a not very popular pastime, to say the least, with enthusiasm soon waning, thus leaving a dedicated core to complete the arduous work. Indeed, it was to take a number of years to complete this section to operational condition.

The Second and Third Stages, to Ballydugan and Inch[5] respectively, would proceed when land acquisition discussions were resolved.

## Signals

Signalling equipment was a very important element in the safe operation of any railway. Its visual impact contributed greatly to the special atmosphere of the Edwardian period and, in particular, the semaphore signals used on the BCDR with their white, lattice steel posts and lower quadrant arms (the signal arm was lowered to allow the train to pass) were very pleasing to behold.

However, due to the modernisation of the railways and the introduction of automatic coloured light signals, this traditional system with its local signal boxes was fast disappearing from the railway landscape and, like the steam engine, was about to disappear forever. No longer would it be possible to stand on the railway platform and see the signal arm drop with that distinctive 'clunk', indicating that the train was due. It was, therefore, very important that we should try to recover as much of this equipment as possible before it was dumped as scrap.

By this time, we had earned a good reputation with NIR, so when signal equipment on the Bangor line, together with the lever-frame in Bangor signal box, become redundant, it was offered to us.

***Above:*** Double bracket signal installed at Downpatrick station.

Thus, in 1988 we were invited by NIR to join a work train which was to be used in the clearance of the redundant signal equipment between Belfast Central station and Bangor. This was a train made up of diesel locomotive No 104, two bogie flat wagons and a 20 ton ballast wagon. The operation took up most of the day, our volunteers helping NIR staff to load the signal posts onto the flat wagons.

It was an interesting experience to travel on the wagons which, between lifts, gave us a very different view of the Bangor line. In addition to the signal posts, other components, including point-roding, pulleys and many other accessories invaluable for the restoration of our signal installation, were also recovered.

However, the main item of equipment we were particularly interested in was the forty lever frame from Bangor signalbox which we intended to install in our 'new' box (when eventually acquired).

From an early stage in the development of our scheme, we had been on the lookout for a suitable signalbox and from time to time our attention was drawn to possible subjects. Those considered initially were Tynan, Larne, Drogheda and Lisburn.

Noel Killen, one of our management committee members, was anxious that we make some progress with this project, as he had a volunteer bricklayer, keen to construct the brick base.

The most appropriate candidate was the North Box situated at Drogheda, Co Louth. We were aware at that time that it had been removed from its brick base but we still had some doubt about its size. On making tentative enquiries it appeared that the box could be donated to us and with this knowledge Noel carried out a site inspection and confirmed its suitability. At this stage a member of the Society was prepared to pay the £300 transport costs. Unfortunately, however, so great were the financial pressures on us at that time, that the Management Committee asked if it would be possible to defer this purchase and use the £300 offer instead for the purchase and transportation of an operational carriage from CIÉ, which was regarded as being much more urgent. It was to be another five years and many inspections of other signal boxes including Carrickfergus and Craigavad, before a suitable one became available.

Finally, by early 1991, our long search was ended when NIR agreed to let us dismantle the now redundant LMS NCC signal box at King's Bog, on the Bleach Green to Antrim line and which had controlled the branch line to Ballyclare a few miles to the north of Belfast. Although this branch closed in 1950 (the same year as the closure of the BCDR), the box finally ceased to have any function in 1981.

What a good choice this proved to be, due to its many positive features, and well worth waiting for. Its scale was just right for our location, it had windows on all four sides allowing excellent viewing of our whole site, and it was big enough to accommodate large groups of people, such as a class of school children. In addition, it had a fireplace cleverly designed into one corner which avoided intrusion into the main body of the room. Needless to say, this box was to become a popular place for some of our volunteers during cold winter months.

The building itself was in excellent condition too, consisting of a red brick base with two windows. The lower space housed the main machinery which transferred the actions of the upper levers to the track and signals.

The upper portion of the building was of timber construction, 90% of which was glazed. The roof was finished with Bangor Blue slates with the large overhang, thus affording excellent protection to the windows below. This particular roof feature was, of course, typical of the LMS NCC and quite different to normal BCDR practice, but we felt that this design variation could be regarded as 'poetic licence'.

We were fortunate that our Infrastructure Officer, Jim Carson, was prepared to take on the task of dismantling and rebuilding the box with the able assistance of a small team of volunteers[6].

***Above:*** The ex-NCC signal cabin at Kingsbog Junction, in course of dismantling.     *Drew Sucksmith*

**Left:** The signal box during reconstruction in 1993.

*Drew Sucksmith*

**Right:** The signal box in the final stages of rebuilding: James Carson, David Crone and Jim Carson.

**Left:** The signal box in 1993, after completion.

*Drew Sucksmith*

In common with the other buildings on our site, the location of the new signalbox was dictated by the usual constraints, viz, a pressurised sewer, ground conditions, track layout and in this particular case, visibility. The signalman had to be able to see the whole area controlled by his box.

Although ground conditions were expected to be poor, to our relief, the engineers were confident that deep, conventional strip foundations would be satisfactory, as the proposed building was not excessively, heavy having 90% windows on the first floor.

Since completion in 1996, this exhibit has proved to be very popular with our visitors, in particular children, who get great pleasure in operating the signal levers. These are specific levers not connected to the system therefore eliminating any possibility of a major disaster! Although the final connections to the signals and points have not yet been completed, it is still the intention to have this box fully operational in the 'fullness of time'.

***Above:*** Antrim water tower.

# Water tower

The extraordinarily wide variety of structures required, in order to allow a working steam railway to function efficiently, is demonstrated by the next project, a water tower.

Early in 1990, NIR offered us the water tower at Antrim Station on the ex LMS NCC line. Although this line was still operational, this facility was no longer required, as the water tower at Ballymena, the next station along the track, would be retained in working order for the use by 'steam specials'.

The recovery was tricky enough, as the tank was the size of a small room perched on top of a column 16 feet (4.8m) above platform level.

Special lifting lugs had been welded on to facilitate lifting by crane after the tank was unbolted from its supporting column. All the work was successfully carried out by our volunteers [7] and moved to Downpatrick for installation at the end of our main platform.

Again, careful consideration had to be given to the design of the foundation, principally due to the weight of water supported at such a height, as well as the poor ground conditions in the area. Our Engineers required a mass concrete foundation of nine foot (2.7m) square by ten foot (3m) deep.

Much preparatory work was necessary to restore this exhibit, due to it being badly corroded internally. It required de-rusting with a needle gun, a very unpleasant and noisy task which had to be carried out inside the tank, a job patiently carried out by Raymond Duggan. I undertook to apply the fibreglass resin to the internal surfaces, having had prior experience when repairing the 'Guinness' locomotive's water tank.

The task of re-erecting the tower was postponed until a crane was required for some other major lift and the job was finally completed, without any problem, at a later date.

An interesting design feature of this structure was that provision was made for keeping the water from freezing during winter frosts by the fitting of a small firebox at the base of the column. The heated air and smoke would rise up the inside of the column and exit through a series of holes directly under the tank.

At first sight, a water tank such as this looks like a very simple structure but, in fact, a lot of practical design and ingenuity by the manufacturers, Cowans Sheldon & Co Ltd of Carlisle, produced a very effective and necessary piece of railway equipment which has stood the test of time.

Both the water tower and signal gantry, which now stand at the end of the main platform, bear a striking resemblance to the original installations, which were a feature of Downpatrick Station until its closure.

## Landscaping

One aspect of railway preservation is that it covers such a wide range of activities, thus allowing scope for volunteers with many varied interests. Landscaping and tree planting was one such activity which we regarded as important, especially at the beginning of our project. We were fortunate to have Tom Page take on this responsibility and, in association with the Conservation Volunteers (CV), over 450 trees were planted during Ulster Tree Week. He was also successful in obtaining grants of £150 and £350 from the CV and Shell respectively.

Tom had to take great care to make certain of selecting those planting areas which would avoid conflict with train operations, ie sight lines and branches too close to the track. The local bird population, such as geese and swans also had to be given consideration with regard to their flight paths. At all times, we kept in focus the main objective, which was to enhance the beautiful views for those passengers in the carriages as the train travelled along the track.

### Footnotes

1   These early pioneers included Cyril & Graham Leathers, Noel & Paul Killen, Jim Perry, Robert Edwards, John Hughes, David Trotter, Martin Lavery, Niall, Feargal & Gerry Cochrane, Hugo Smyth, James Murphy.

2   Camac Clark, Gerry Cochrane, Jim Perry, Cyril and Graham Leathers, Martin Laverty, Tom Page, John Hughes, David Trotter.

3   Walter Burke, Michael Collins.

4   See chapter 8

5   See chapter 7

6   Noel Killen, Jim & James Carson, John Reilly.

7   Richard Convery, David Trotter, Mike Collins.

***Above:*** GS&WR 0-6-0T No 90 avails of the water tower in 2008.

## CHAPTER 6
# GRAND DESIGNS

The year 1988 began with the design and location of the permanent buildings that were required, namely a workshop, station building and platform. This marked an interesting stage in our development which, when completed, would make a terrific difference to our facilities for maintenance and restoration. In addition, it would allow us to offer much improved facilities to visitors and help to create an entrance with an Edwardian atmosphere. I agreed to act as architect on a voluntary basis, and set about preparing sketch plans and all necessary approvals. Preparation of detailed drawings, contract documents and supervision of the contract would occupy most of my free time during this period.

## Workshop

This building was required to provide facilities for restoration and repair of locomotives and carriages, together with room for all the heavy machinery associated with metal and woodwork. A minimum of two tracks was essential, each having an inspection pit to facilitate access to the underside of vehicles. Its external appearance was expected to be in keeping with the railway architecture of the early twentieth century.

Difficult site conditions had a fundamental effect and created two major constraints relating to the size and design of the building. The first was the presence of an 18 inch (450mm) diameter pressurised sewer which crossed the compound diagonally from a position behind the signal box to the bottom left hand side of the car park. The building had to be at least 16 feet (5m) clear of this, effectively leaving a triangular site for the location of the Workshop, a major factor in determining the maximum size of the building.

The second limitation was the nature of the sub-soil, composed of peat to a depth of 90 feet (21m). This ruled out the possibility of any type of solid masonry construction, due to the cost of necessary piling. Therefore, a lightweight, steel frame structure with metal cladding to walls and roof was the only practical solution. The whole building would float on a reinforced concrete raft which would distribute the loads over the whole surface of the ground.

A timber frame and cladding, similar to the goods shed at Castlewellan station would have been an alternative, but this carried a risk of fire and vandalism.

***Above:*** The author in front of the workshop frame.

*Bill Hagan*

***Left:*** The Gas
Works manager's
house on the
original site.

The overall design of the workshop was based on the BCDR goods shed at Newtownards, which has since been demolished. Although this was a stone building with red sandstone linings to the entrance arches and circular vents in the gable apexes, the general effect was reproduced with the use of metal cladding. The large timber doors, bolts and strap hinges are exact reproductions of those in the former Newtownards shed. It was agreed that no heating would be provided, as the building was not to be insulated and so the heating costs would have been extremely high.

## Station Building

The original station building in Downpatrick was located in the centre of Market Street, approximately where the present library now stands. Surprisingly, it was constructed in red brick but was otherwise unremarkable in appearance and it was demolished in the early seventies.

While considering my approach to the design of the new station building, my feeling was that it should reflect the Edwardian period rather than a modern design. With this in mind, my attention was attracted to a derelict building situated on the opposite side of Market Street.

Originally the gasworks manager's house, it had been gutted by fire some years previously but was of the correct period and scale and would be ideal if it could be moved to our site.

When I approached the owner, Mr Brendan Rodgers, and explained my 'grand design' for his building, he reacted with some initial shock but later indicated that he would be prepared to donate the building to us. What was required was the stonework of the front façade and the chimney pots. All the roof timbers and slates had been destroyed in the fire and there was nothing else worth saving.

The building had been built in 1846 as part of the gasworks complex, when street lighting was first introduced, just 13 years before the railway arrived, on the 23 March 1859. Its main façade was built of roughly dressed whinstone with sandstone quoins. Window and door openings had been lined with dressed sandstone while the arched entrance was topped with a pediment of sandstone to match the coping stones.

As this was a 'listed' building, approval from the Historic Building Branch of the DOE would be necessary before any demolition could be considered, although I was fairly confident that approval would be given on the understanding that the building would be rebuilt on our site, externally exactly as the original.

Perhaps a year after my discussion with Mr Rodgers, I discovered that the gasworks house had, in the interim, been sold to the SEELB. This was a complete surprise to me, particularly as I worked for the Board at that time. However, I was not too concerned about this development and preceded with the design of our station building based on the gasworks house.

I asked the SEELB if they would consider donating the building to our museum, pointing out that the building which they had acquired was in a dangerous condition, was a listed building which they could not demolish, was taking up valuable room on their restricted site and was an eyesore. I informed them that we could probably acquire listed building consent to allow the building to be moved and rebuilt on our site.

It was obvious that this arrangement would be to the advantage of all concerned and was duly approved by their Board who arranged to have the stones numbered, dismantled and transported for storage on our site.

Once more, site restrictions such as ground conditions, track alignment and, in this case a boundary drain, had to be considered in the positioning of the building.

Because this was going to be a heavy masonry building and, as already explained, piling was out of the question, traditional strip foundations would be required. Therefore,

the building had to be located as close to the bottom of Cathedral Hill as possible as, the closer to the hill, the better the ground and therefore the more shallow the foundations that would be required. The second, and equally limiting, problem was the alignment of the track. The layout had to accommodate a run round loop (double track) with a minimum curvature of ten chains and this curve had to link up with the track entering the station area.

Test holes were required to confirm that reasonable foundations could be found; otherwise it was back to the drawing board. The holes were dug with a JCB in the presence of the structural engineer and I can still recall the suspense at the time. So much depended on a favourable result. As the digging got deeper, with no sign of improvement, I was beginning to despair. At a depth of seven feet (2.1m) the bucket was still bringing up peat, a situation which could not continue much longer, I thought. Then at eight feet (2.4m) the situation improved and the engineer was satisfied that traditional, though deep, mass concrete foundations were indeed possible. There was quite a sense of relief all round but the excessive depth had cost implications for the future.

The exterior of the building would be exactly the same as the original, the only difference being that the ground floor level would be at platform level, approximately one metre

**Right:** The station building in March 1990, during the reconstruction.

*Drew Sucksmith*

***Left:*** The completed and landscaped station building.

above ground level, thus necessitating steps up to the front entrance.

Internally, the arrangement would be planned to suit the requirements of our station building, with the ground floor housing a booking hall, shop, ticket office, visitors' toilets and stationmaster's room. On the first floor, there was to be an exhibition room and office.

After much delay due to the difficulty of obtaining possession of our site, work was finally ready to begin on the construction of the workshop and station building. However, before this could occur, some disruption to our other activities, and additional work by our volunteers, would be required. Unfortunately, by this stage the Enterprise Ulster scheme had ended, which left volunteers under great pressure to complete the preliminary works in time to allow this contract to begin in May.

Our temporary platform had to be dismantled and further temporary boarding facilities provided, to allow our public operations to continue without interruption.

After all the hassle and headaches which arose during construction, it was a great period for us all to eventually take possession of these buildings and prepare them for their future use. Because of the cost-cutting requirements in the building contracts, volunteers had to complete some of the work themselves, such as additional electrical work, together with the internal painting of the station building before the official opening.

DDC undertook to landscape the front of the station with roses and various ground cover planting. The provision of two hanging baskets at the front entrance was the icing on the cake and the result was very impressive.

## The Grand Opening

May Day 1990 was another very significant date in the history of our museum for on this day we celebrated in great style the formal opening.

As this occasion was going to be the most significant event that we would ever experience, we wanted to celebrate in the traditional railway fashion. We therefore decided to have a banquet in the large, new workshop. Brunel would have approved!

In a very generous gesture on his part, Ciaran McAteer, our Chairman, decided to stand down and allow me to act as Chairman during this period. I appreciated this very much. For me, at least, this event marked the culmination of many years of hard struggle to fulfil a dream, so I was keen that everything would go smoothly.

Consideration had to be given to working out details such the overall plan of events from the arrival of the guest

*Left:* The arrival of the Guests of Honour at the official opening of the new station, 1 May 1990.

*Mourne Observer*

of honour and cutting the ribbon, location of the banquet, menu, caterers, guest list, entertainment, train formation, timetable and date. Guests were to be encouraged to come in period costume to add to the occasion.

We were delighted when Lord Dunleath made it known that he would be willing to perform the opening ceremony and so the big day began with our guest of honour having driven from the Mall through the town in an open horse-drawn carriage to be greeted on arrival at the station by a reception committee composed of the Chairman of DDC, Mr Michael Boyd and Mrs Boyd, together with myself as Chairman of the Railway and my wife, Roisin. After a few words of welcome, guests were ushered into the station and on to the platform, where the Guinness locomotive was sitting hissing away, resplendent in her recently painted deep blue livery. Even Nature smiled on us, providing a glorious sunny morning.

Coupled to the locomotive were an open wagon and a brake van, at that time our only 'passenger' vehicles. Entertainment was provided by an excellent brass band named 'Downbeat' – a group of seven students from Down High School who occupied the open wagon in the centre of the train. We were all feeling so proud and elated and the period costumes of the guests, with Lord Dunleath in full morning suit and top hat, added greatly to the grandeur of the occasion.

Without any further encouragement, Lord Dunleath leapt onto the footplate with the enthusiasm of a twelve year-old. After a few words to the happy throng of guests gathered on the platform, he opened the regulator and with

*Above:* The open wagon where entertainment was provided by 'Downbeat'.

*Above:* Lord Dunleath on the footplate of *Guinness*.

*Down Recorder*

a loud whistle from *Guinness*, drove the train through the tape declaring our railway open. I shall never forget my emotional feelings at that time. All the work and previous worry faded and I thought how wonderful it was to be part of such a team. No doubt my colleagues had similar thoughts.

Meanwhile, in the workshop, tables for over 140 guests had been dressed for the opening banquet. The stark workshop had been transformed and suitably decorated for the guests, who included local politicians, officers and Councillors of DDC, representatives from the IDB

***Below:*** At the official opening, left to right standing: Alan and Muriel Major, the author, Lord Dunleath, Roisin Cochrane, Mike Collins, Jim Perry and Bill Gillespie.

Seated: James Perry and Aoife Collins.

(Japanese section) NITB, DED, and RPSI, together with our volunteers and their wives and partners.

During his speech, Lord Dunleath was generous in his praise of our effort and remarked that it showed how one can sometimes achieve the impossible, noting however that miracles take a little longer, thus referring to our plan to cross the Ballydugan Road. He went on to express his good wishes and hopes for the future and in his usual generous manner, made a presentation of £1,000 to assist in our future development work.

In reply, Mr Boyd on behalf of the Council also praised our efforts and promised continuing support.

In my speech of reply, having first expressed our thanks to our guest of honour, I also singled out our Japanese friends with a few words of thanks in Japanese, which drew a round of applause.

All that remained was for the fun to begin and, after a splendid meal, guests were treated to train rides back and forth to the Loop Platform for the remainder of the afternoon.

By all accounts, the event was a great success and Lord Dunleath, in a letter to

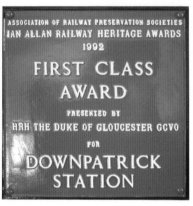

me a few days later, thanked us for a most memorable day.

As a postscript, some months after this event I received a serious request from a senior DDC officer inquiring if we would consider the idea of demolishing the station and building a new one some distance to the north of our present compound. My first reaction was that this was a joke. My second reaction is not printable here nor did I refer the request to our Directors as I thought that their reply would have been even more colourful than mine.

This arose because at this time the Council was anxious to find a site suitable for the proposed St Patrick's Heritage Centre, which was eventually sited in the Grove.

Two years after this memorable event, the station building received a First Class Award which is an annual award sponsored by the Railway Heritage Trust and Ian Allan Ltd. In addition to the award, a cheque for £750 was presented by HRH, the Duke of Gloucester. A handsome cast aluminium plaque marking the event is now proudly displayed in the booking hall.

*Above:* Maghera station in 1995. On the left is the station building and, in the distance, the goods store, now at Downpatrick.

## New engine shed

Although our new station building had been in operation for a number of years and was fulfilling its new function to the satisfaction of both our own members and visitors alike, I was aware that one important element was missing, a platform canopy. I had been on the lookout for a suitable canopy for a number of years and was delighted when Mark Kennedy of the UFTM contacted me in 1995 with news of one at Maghera station situated on the former Derry Central Railway in County Londonderry. This canopy was part of the former goods shed, a large stone building, owned by the DOE Roads Service. It had just been sold to a developer and its demolition was now imminent.

An inspection confirmed that the canopy

***Above:*** A model of the proposed new loco shed, made by the author for approval by the Board of Directors.

would be ideal for our purpose as its scale was in keeping with our own station building. It was a three-bay structure with four cast iron columns supporting a flat roof formed with pitch pine beams and fascia boarding.

Further inquiries revealed that the canopy could be released to us on one condition, which was that we take the stone goods shed as well! My initial reaction was one of shock but I soon realised that a great opportunity had dropped in our lap.

The building in question was built in 1880 of coursed basalt rubble with internal dimensions of 79ft by 29.5ft (24m by 9m). On one side, a cantilever roof covered the loading bay, while the other side had a three-bay canopy. The main roof was originally decked with corrugated iron, supported on composite trusses of wrought iron ties, cast iron struts and pitch pine rafters.

This was typical railway goods shed construction, similar to the goods shed in Ardglass and would be an excellent exhibit in its own right, as well as adding to our railway heritage.

At about this time, we had been considering the construction of a locomotive shed and my immediate thought was that this goods shed would be ideal. After all, we had already successfully moved one stone building. The usual problems loomed – no money and no time. Our Board of Directors gave approval, on condition that suitable funding could be obtained. The estimated cost of transporting the materials – viz stone, roof trusses and roof timbers – to Downpatrick was £2,500 which, at the eleventh hour was provided by Downpatrick Project Board.

Before demolition could begin, I had to carry out a detailed survey of the building to allow me to prepare the

construction drawings that would be required for the various stages of reconstruction. These were to obtain Planning and Building Control approvals, together with approvals from the various funding bodies.

This proposed new engine shed would have two roads (tracks) with inspection pits and locomotive access from both ends. The three-bay canopy, of course, would be re-erected over the station platform.

After all preparation work was completed, the building was dismantled in September 1995, with much appreciated co-operation from the staff of DOE Roads Service in Maghera. All the materials, twenty lorry loads of stone and three loads of timber, were moved to Downpatrick to await re-building whenever funding became available.

It was to take another 18 months before all the grants were approved, a delay which was to have unfortunate consequences on the smooth progress of the building contract, as explained in detail in Chapter 8.

The usual foundation problems had to be addressed, though in this case, with heavy masonry walls, there was no question of any solution other than piling. For the reasons explained in Chapter 8, the building works would be carried out under two separate contracts.

The initial contract, including piling, reinforced concrete floor and inspection pits, would be followed by the main contract. This was completed in May 1999.

Volunteers, as usual, had to finish the work, including internal painting, laying of rails, additional electrical work and external track connections.

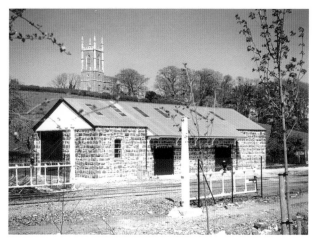

***Above:*** The finished loco shed.

CHAPTER 7
# INCH-BY-INCH

At an early stage in this project it had become obvious to the Directors that the original proposal to extend the railway across the Ballydugan Road in the direction of Ardglass was now looking unrealistic and that a more meaningful alternative destination was urgently required. This view was also shared by DDC's Tourism and Recreation Officer, together with consultants recruited by the Council to advise on the future of tourism in Down District.

The only practical alternatives were to extend the track westward to Ballydugan corn mill and also north across the Quoile River to Inch Abbey, both of which were favoured by the NITB In the short term, the Ballydugan option was frustrated by problems over land acquisition so the Abbey extension appeared to offer the better potential.

Initial discussions between David Trotter and the landowner, farmer John Kennedy, were encouraging, eventually leading to an agreement in principle, the valuation to be determined later by the District Valuer.

The Cistercian abbey at Inch was built in 1100 AD by John De Courcy. It is located about one mile north of Downpatrick and set in extensive wooded grounds on the banks of the Quoile River. The abbey was closed on the orders of King Henry VIII in his infamous dissolution of the monasteries campaign and is now a ruin of great splendour situated in a spectacular setting. This historic monument

***Above:*** Gate Lodge beside Inch Abbey in 1959, with my future wife at the gate.

does not attract the visitor interest it deserves and is largely a hidden gem, owned and maintained by the Historic Buildings Branch of the DOE.

It was generally believed that our proposed link with the abbey would greatly enhance the railway as a tourist attraction, increase the abbey's tourism profile as well as providing a meaningful link with Down Cathedral and St Patrick's Heritage Centre. This would be an attractive package to offer tourists when visiting Down District.

However, we realised that the construction of this extension would be a formidable undertaking, involving the reinstatement of track from our North Junction to the Quoile River followed by a new track formation over a former landfill site. A platform with a run round loop would also have to be built near the abbey car park. An existing derelict gate lodge at the abbey entrance was to be restored as a waiting room for visitors.

By a remarkable coincidence, forty years previously in 1959, I had taken a photograph of this same gate lodge with my fiancée posed at the garden gate. I had no connection whatever with this particular building and it was just by pure chance that I included it in the photograph.

The most expensive element, however, would be the construction of a new steel girder bridge over the River Quoile.

The original bridge, known locally as the Pile Bridge, was built in 1859, for the opening of the line. It was constructed with lattice trusses on piles and was replaced in 1930 with steel girders, supported on a single central pier with concrete abutments at either end, giving a total overall length of 140 feet in two spans. The steel girders were removed shortly after the railway closed but, fortunately, from our point of view, the central pier and abutments remained intact and in good condition.

## Making a start

In order to promote this ambitious project and explore costs and funding, a sub-committee was set up. Progress was good and by March 1997 we had obtained approval in principle from the IFI with the understanding that they would provide 90% of the total cost, the remainder to be provided by DDC (see chapter 8).

With the various problems of funding now sorted out, concern was mounting over the time being taken by DDC in the drafting of the formal agreement between the Council and the Railway Company, which was required by the IFI before their grant could be formally approved.

Remarkably, it was to take another four years for DDC to get the legal arrangements for the land acquisition sorted out. "It was not a high priority" I was told! Part of the delay was also due to a last minute concern by the landowner regarding trains operating on Sundays. Thankfully, after protracted discussions, this problem was eventually solved.

A further late requirement by the landowner for additional accommodation works, the cost of which had to be absorbed within our existing budget, resulted in the abandonment of our plans for the restoration of the gate lodge.

It should be recorded that, in spite of the above, our dealings with the landowner, Mr John Kennedy, have always been exceptionally good and remain so to this day.

In anticipation of the Inch extension proceeding, a small permanent way team[1] had been established some months earlier with plans to extend the track from our Home Junction to the North Junction. This work, carried out mid-week in order not to interfere with the track laying currently under way on the west line on Saturdays was, even with the assistance of a JCB, a slow and business. Due to subsidence of the original track bed, which had occurred during the intervening 50 years since the railway closed, the new track

*Above:* The author, setting out the alignment for new track to Inch.

bed had to be raised by approximately two feet.

In the summer of 1998 an advanced party, consisting of myself, David and Dessie, moved on to the Inch Abbey site to mark out boundaries and establish the exact route of the track where it veered to the right off the original alignment of the main line to Belfast.

*Above:* Setting out boundaries are David Trotter and Dessie Morrison.

I remember this period very well because the weather was exceptionally hot, with undergrowth reaching way above our heads and clegs hungry for our blood. We persevered in the knowledge that we were now about to construct a completely new section of railway, the first on the BCDR since the building of the Ardglass Branch in 1892. We were railway pioneers!

As soon as we had established the boundaries, fencing work began, carried out by a specialist fencing contractor as required by a condition in our lease. It was followed immediately by stripping off the topsoil in readiness for the laying of 'Geogrid', a plastic mesh membrane. This was necessary, as the ground was originally a landfill site and so subject to uneven settlement.

The next stage was the construction of the track formation, (the foundation for the concrete sleepers) which required 5,000 tons of stone to be spread and levelled. For this operation we hired a tracked excavator and driver and, as well as spreading the stone, the machine effectively compacted the material, which was an added bonus.

I can recall with great clarity the first morning of this operation, when I was expecting the excavator and stone lorries to arrive on site. At eight o'clock on a cold January morning, when I arrived on site, only the first hint of day break was showing. It was indeed a bleak morning, teeming with rain and I could just barely make out the outline of six loaded lorries sitting there waiting for directions. My immediate reaction was – "Why on earth am I doing this?" However, there was now no turning back, so it was on with the boots and a start made at organising the unloading of the lorries in the general direction of Inch Abbey. For the remainder of that day an endless stream of vehicles, each loaded with 20 tons of stone, kept arriving at 15 minute intervals, an operation which was to continue during the following week.

By the end of the year the track formation was ready for the setting out of the sleepers but, before this could be undertaken, there was one minor detail to be considered – bridging the River Quoile.

## Bridging the gap

It was my original intention that the construction of the Inch Abbey extension would be carried out by civil engineering contractors thus leaving only the track laying

***Above:*** The loaded lorries wait for directions on a cold January dawn.

to be carried out by our volunteers.

However, when tenders were received, it was obvious that the original estimate of the cost, on which our budget was based, was much too low and, therefore, the contract as intended could not proceed (see Chapter 8).

The only possible option, therefore, was for all work, with the exception of the steel girder bridge, to be carried out by ourselves, an enormous task given the amount of labour and organisation involved. For our workers, few in number, many of whom were well beyond retirement age and all without experience in this type of work, it was going to be a long struggle and a steep learning curve.

The final arrangements therefore were as follows:-

1  Girder Bridge to be fabricated and installed by a specialist contractor under the supervision of our Structural Consultants.

2  Farm access road and boundary fencing to be carried out as minor works contracts by outside contractors, under my supervision.

3  The remainder of the works to be undertaken by ourselves, again with my involvement and supervision. This work included the following:-

•  Setting out the new track alignment.
•  Preparing the new track formation.
•  Preparing the access for the bridge girders.
•  Carrying out the accommodation works for the bridge contract.
•  Realignment of bridge embankments.
•  Trackwork.

***Right:*** Inspection Posse October 1998: L-R Ian Davis, Arthur Muskett, Nelson Heron, Barney Graham, Robert Gardiner, John Reilly, Mike Collins, Alan Major, Colin Holliday, George Legg, John Henry, Edwin Gray, Desmond Morrison, Edward Duly, David Trotter, Richard Convery.

- Construction of the platform at Inch.
- Construction of timber walkway.
- Construction of pedestrian footpath.
- Culverts.
- Level-crossings.

With this increased responsibility, I asked our Board of Directors and Management Committee for their full co-operation during this very demanding period. In order to carry out this work efficiently and within a reasonable time scale, the Board, at their meeting in December 1997, agreed that I should act as Project Manager with David Trotter acting as Assistant Manager. David Crone agreed to be Engineering Advisor.

With the contract for the bridge having been signed in August 1998 and completion expected before the end of the year, the volunteers were now under considerable pressure to have the accommodation works completed in time for the delivery of the bridge girders.

***Above:*** Inch Abbey, October 1998. Excavated track bed with geogrid reinforcement.

One of the main difficulties regarding the construction of this bridge was that of access for the 70 foot long steel girders, two of which were required at each side of the river. Among the suggestions proposed by our engineers was the possibility of floating the girders on suitable rafts from the Belfast Road up river. I suggested moving them by rail from the Downpatrick end as the track could then be completed as far as the river by that time.

In the event, it was decided to transport the girders to the north and south banks by road using extendable trailers. This solution was anything but straightforward because on the north approach, access was particularly torturous, consisting of many sharp bends and narrow farm lanes on raised embankments. It would be necessary for us, therefore, to remove gates, ease bends and finally reinstate everything on completion, all of which added greatly to the volunteer workload and expense.

On the south approach access was reasonably straightforward as it would follow the original track bed, the only problem here being that concrete sleepers had already been laid on most of this section and these would now have to be lifted and set aside. Fortunately, this work could be accomplished with the assistance of our JCB.

In addition to all of this, the main item of accommodation works was the provision for a hard-standing platform to support a 125 ton crane at each end of the bridge.

The specification given to me by the crane company indicated that they would require a temporary stone platform approximately 30 feet square at track bed level (ten feet above ground level and graded at a minimum of 45 degrees). I was staggered at the quantity of stone which was going to be required, 300 tons of quarry-face rubble (ungraded stone from dust to stones as large as three feet). Obviously the assistance of the track excavator would be required to build and grade the platforms but the extra cost of all this additional work was causing me some concern.

At last, by early December, most of the accommodation works had been completed and the date for the installation of the bridge was set for 2 January 1999.

## Spanner in the works

Exactly seven days before the bridge steelwork was due to arrive on site, and with all arrangements made, I was told that we did not have approval from the Rivers Authority to put a bridge across the river. This sounded pretty serious and I immediately had visions of ending up with two railways and a gap in the middle. After the initial panic and telephone calls to Eddie McGrady, the Rivers Authority quickly carried out a site inspection and proclaimed that our proposal was satisfactory.

Installation actually began on 16 January and was a nail-biting occasion for the contractor and myself. My particular concerns were access for the longest lorry in Ireland and whether the hard-standing was sufficiently compacted to take the 125 ton crane when lifting the 70 foot long, by six foot high, steel girders.

The bridge contractor was concerned about the wind strength and the effect this would have on controlling the girder during the lift. In order to assist with this problem it was decided to attach a rope to one end of the girder with the other end fixed to our JCB under the control of driver, Phil McGivern.

In total, four days were required to complete the bridge and during the course of the work, a safety boat was in attendance on the river in case anybody slipped and fell in. In the event, all our anxieties turned out to be groundless and I was relieved that this safety feature was not required.

The original track alignment had a slight curve, resulting in a kink in the centre of the bridge. As replicating this would have reduced clearances for some of our modern

***Above:*** The tricky bit – getting the girders to the river!

***Left:*** The Quoile bridge in January 1999, as the first girder was placed.

*Author*

***Below left:*** The second girder joins the first.

*Drew Sucksmith*

be brought up to the bridge on our work train. Securing these sleepers in position on the steel bridge beams was a nervous affair for David and Dessie, as one false move could have resulted in an unscheduled swim in the Quoile. The problem was that each sleeper had to be screwed from below, requiring whoever was doing the work to stand on a temporary platform suspended above the water.

## Helping hand

It was recognised by those of us involved in the hard, physical work of track laying that if we were to proceed efficiently, we would need a better method of handling concrete sleepers.

After some hours at the drawing board I produced a design for a sleeper gantry, a low four-wheeled wagon with an overhead beam projecting fore and aft which would allow a chain hoist to travel from one end to the other carrying one sleeper. It was discussed with David and we tossed ideas around regarding its improvement and detail design.

carriages, it was decided to install the new bridge with a straight alignment, an action which resulted in the realignment of the embankments on the approaches to the bridge. A major bonus gained from this was that we were able to make use of all the stone used in the construction of the temporary crane platforms.

The completion of the bridge was a great boost to morale and no time was wasted in getting started on the trackwork which would eventually see us to Inch Abbey.

With the renewed vigour gained, it was not long before the track was laid as far as the Quoile and the new timber sleepers which had been ordered from England could now

As luck would have it, some time later David came across a derelict track gantry hidden amongst the weeds in a turf bog in the south of Ireland. It had previously been used by Bord na Mona when handling panels of their three foot gauge track. He thought it was very similar to our own proposed design and indeed it turned out to be a very lucky find. When converted to our five foot three gauge, it was to completely transform our sleeper handling operations beyond all recognition. However, when this rather decrepit piece of equipment first arrived on site I detected some scepticism and amusement among some volunteers about its

*Above:* Re-aligned embankment at the Quoile Bridge.

usefulness and our ability to make it operational.

This gantry, together with two bogies which we built to carry the sleepers, made the work of track laying a joy to carry out. It could accommodate 20 concrete sleepers as well as eight 20 foot temporary rails, sufficient to lay one 60 foot panel of track. In addition, it could handle the very long and heavy timbers required in the construction of turnouts. By this stage, too, our permanent way team had been boosted by additional volunteers[2] who were a very welcome addition to the work-force.

Another very useful acquisition to our range of equipment, when we were eventually permitted to use it, was a Wickham inspection vehicle, again acquired by David. This machine

*Above:* Laying turnout timbers – Sleeper gantry at Inch. Barney Graham, Dessie Morrison, John Henry and Andy Cook.

could tow our two bogies loaded with all our tools. This was a small, four-wheel vehicle with a diesel engine and had the additional advantage of providing shelter from the elements when working away from base. However, it did have one drawback in that it was limited in its ability to move the heavier loads now required. This duty was eventually taken over by one of our G class diesel locomotives as it had sufficient power to pull the sleeper-gantry together with the fully loaded trucks. A frequent duty also included the movement of two fully loaded 10 ton ballast wagons and a 20 ton brake van.

## The end is nigh

By Christmas 2003 we were ready to begin the construction of the platform at Inch and it was clear that, with a determined push, there was a very good chance that we could have the whole Inch Abbey extension completed and operational for the 2004 summer season, which would be a tremendous boost to the entire scheme. I had worked out a detailed programme for the completion of all the outstanding work, indicating that this goal was reasonably achievable. As a result, our General Manager, Edwin Gray, decided that we should give this top priority. His decision was not welcomed at the time by David who felt he was being put under too much pressure. However, the NITB were leaning heavily on us to complete, threatening to withdraw our grant, so I was determined that we should at least try and see how far we could get.

From this point onwards David backed off and I had to take over the day-to-day management. This was a big blow and one regretted by all the permanent way team, not least by myself. David and I had been a very effective team for many years and it was our first major disagreement. His input had been invaluable and I knew he would be a big loss.

Up to this point David had been both our locomotive and JCB driver, functions which were in daily demand for loading and driving the work train. The driving duty now had to be taken over by John Henry with Paul McMullan acting as standby driver. With regard to the JCB, this problem was solved when I asked our professional driver, Phil McGivern, to give me some lessons in its operation. This was a new skill for me but a very necessary one in the new circumstances.

*Above:* The Quoile bridge in 2008.     *Norman Johnston*

## Platform construction

To construct the platform at Inch Abbey a special works train was created, consisting of a 60 foot bogie underframe and our GS&WR brake van. The underframe was decked with timber sleepers thus providing a working platform to accommodate sand, stones, cement, water tank and cement mixer. Concrete for the foundations was to be mixed on board. The brake van was used to carry tools and materials which required a degree of security but its main attraction was that it provided mess accommodation and shelter from the elements. We had already spent some months preparing the van for this duty. The roof was re-covered, windows glazed with 10mm thick polycarbonate salvaged by Dessie from a skip. An unusually high degree of comfort was provided by upholstered bench seats which were salvaged by John Reilly from a scrapped ambulance. All this, together with a gas heater, was unheard of opulence on the DAR.

The track layout at Inch station was planned to have two platform faces. The north face (Platform 1) would be the main platform with a run-round loop. The south face (Platform 2) would be a bay platform with one track and a buffer stop at the end.

In order to facilitate work on the construction of the platform, the main line track to Platform 1 was laid first, carefully aligned and levelled, thus providing a reference point for the exact location and height of the platform deck. With the track now permanently installed along platform one, the works train could be positioned exactly where required.

Due to the fact that this whole area had been the local Council's landfill site for domestic rubbish, the design of the platform had to be of a light construction and able to accommodate some ground movement during its lifetime. I considered that the most suitable design would therefore be a timber deck on timber beams supported on steel posts (redundant rail) on concrete foundation pads.

This type of construction, together with our novel working arrangements proved to be very convenient for our

*Above:* Platform construction team. L-R: Desmond Morrison, John Henry, George Legg, Ian Davis, Phil McGivern, George Walker

*Right:* Construction of the platform at Inch. Ian Davis, Camac Clarke, Alan Major, John Henry and Barney Graham at work.

*Below:* Pedestrian bridge at Inch. Works train in the background, with Barney Graham mixing cement. Ian Davis and John Henry are at work.

While this work was going on, serious consideration was given to acquiring additional turnouts, three of which would be required, one for the bay platform and two for the run round loop. By a lucky coincidence, NIR were preparing to clear their site at Fortwilliam, Belfast, in preparation for a major development and with the assistance of Chris McMurry of NIR, we were able to acquire five complete sets.

The recovery of these turnouts was a mammoth task undertaken by David (who was still involved on the periphery), with the assistance of Dessie Morrison and John Henry over a period of two weeks.

With the platform now complete, the only remaining work before the first public train could operate was to provide a pedestrian link from the platform to the Abbey Avenue, which would involve the construction of a footpath and pedestrian footbridge over a small stream. This was

volunteers but, nevertheless, very hard work. Fifty-six concrete pads, each measuring three feet by three feet, nine inches deep, had to be cast in situ. To facilitate this, timber shuttering was prepared first, to allow six pads to be cast per working day. This shuttering was bolted together to be dismantled the following day and set up again for the next six pads. Concrete was mixed on the works train and delivered down a chute directly into each box or into a wheelbarrow for the outer pads.

**Left:** Works train near Inch. On board are Barney Graham, John Reilly, David Trotter, Bill Brown, George Legg and John Henry.

completed by the end of June, allowing limited public operations to commence. It was our intention to complete the run-round loop after the operating season ended.

## Trouble ahead

In June, a few weeks before we were due to open to the public, David expressed doubts about the safety of the turnout on the approach to Platform One. I could see nothing wrong, provided it was clipped and locked to give a straight run through to the platform.

In order to resolve this difficulty between us, a site meeting was arranged with the Health and Safety Executive NI who inspected the whole line from Downpatrick to Inch, paying particular attention to the turnout in question. On completion of their inspection they confirmed that there was no reason to suspend the public opening, so with this good news I went away on holiday at the beginning of July, fully expecting trains to be in full swing at the beginning of the summer season.

It was quite a shock, on my return in mid-August, to find that the opening had been postponed and the line unlikely to be opened before the end of the summer season. After all the efforts and hard work of the construction team, this was indeed very disappointing. The explanation which I received was that the Management Committee meeting (from which I was absent) was given to understand that the turnout still required attention.

In order to try to salvage something from the situation an urgent meeting took place with the HSENI, our Chairman, Mike Collins and myself, to try and resolve the situation. HSENI were happy to confirm their earlier approval and expressed some surprise that the opening had been postponed. The result of this was that we got under way the final weekend of the season. It did help to revive morale and, more particularly, placated the Northern Ireland Tourist Board who by this stage had issued us with a notice of withdrawal of grant due to excessive delay.

For the past year I had been under considerable pressure from the NITB (agents for the IFI) to get this project finished and I was not altogether surprised to receive an ultimatum stating that if the project was not completed by the 1 December 2004 they would have no choice but to withhold the remaining grant and return the monies to the IFI. This was not an unreasonable action because the grant had been approved ten years earlier in 1994! I was now in the happy position of being able to inform them that we had opened the project to the public in September and, although not yet fully completed, I was able to give them a detailed programme for the full completion by May 2005. This went a long way to gaining a stay of execution.

The outstanding work comprised the aligning, levelling and final ballasting of the run round loop, as well as provision of a headshunt and buffer stop. The installation of a third turnout to serve Platform 2 (the bay platform) had to be included also at this stage, although this was not part of the original grant.

The levelling of the run round loop was a very labour intensive task, as the track level had to be raised by approximately 600mm (two feet) over a length of 300 feet. It had to be carried out in lifts of 100mm (four inches) by

*Left:* Ballast wagon derailed, with John Henry (driver) and Dessie Morrison

jacking the track and hand packing the ballast under each sleeper. Towards the end of this process, which took about two months of hard labour, and during the final stage of levelling the headshunt at the end of the line, we had our first disaster.

## That sinking feeling

The headshunt at this time was on an embankment about 1.8m (six feet) above ground level and situated on a marsh. We were gradually raising the track to its final level and had a gradient of about 1 in 30 over the final 15m (50 feet). In order to deliver the ballast to where it was required, as close to the end of the track as possible, the works train with the loaded ten-ton ballast wagon had to be propelled carefully down the 1 in 30 gradient.

I took up a position at the bottom of the embankment in readiness to give hand signals to the driver when to stop. As the ballast wagon approached the place where I thought it wise to halt, I give the 'stop' signal, but to my horror, the wagon continued to approach the end of the track and a void. By this time I was waving my hands like a windmill, all to no effect. This scene appeared to me to be happening in slow motion, with the fully loaded ballast wagon approaching the end of the track and disaster almost above my head. On and on it came until finally it ran out of rail and the first set of wheels went over, the ballast wagon ending up towering above me at an angle of 45 degrees.

I'll not record my first comment but I quickly realised that it could have been much worse. At least two wheels were still on the track, not much consolation when I realised that we faced many days of hard work to retrieve the situation.

The next four days consisted of sheer toil for the track-gang, packing, then jacking and making slow progress inch by inch. The situation was exacerbated by the fact that the ground on one side was a marsh thus requiring extensive packing with timber sleepers to spread the load.

Eventually, we had the wheels jacked up level with the rails and after laying bridging rails (there was a gap of about one metre between the end of the rails and the wheels) we coupled the wayward wagon to the train and very carefully towed it back onto the track. A brief period of rejoicing at our achievement was permitted and we all agreed that although this had been an interesting exercise, it should not be repeated.

## Finale

It was now time for the installation of the track to Platform 2, (the bay platform) which involved the removal of two 60 foot panels of track, the installation of a turnout and the laying of track along the platform face.

The removal of the track panels was carried out with the help of Andy Cook and our JCB, concrete sleepers having been set aside for use in the new track. With the site now cleared, the new timbers were loaded on to our track gantry and propelled out to Inch. These timbers ranged in length from 11 feet up to 16 feet and were 12" x 6" in section.

The gantry machine made the handling child's play but when it came to dealing with the ironwork, (rails and crossings), it was a different matter entirely. The weight

***Above***: Nearly there! – Dessie Morrison, Andy Cook and John Henry.

of these various components was too great for our gantry machine and a totally different approach was called for in order to complete the task as quickly and efficiently as possible.

Once again our works train was adapted to cater for this task, the bogie underframe being cleared to give a 60 foot unbroken surface, in order to accommodate the various rail components which make up a turnout. Loading was carried out the previous day using our JCB and carefully organised to facilitate the unloading of each component as required. It was also intended to load a buffer stop, which was to be placed at the end of the headshunt the following morning when we would have the assistance of a large track excavator. Initially, it looked as if the excavator was not going to succeed in lifting the buffer stop onto the train and after many futile attempts I even considered giving up the effort but the enthusiasm of the other members of the team prevailed and success was at last achieved after removing six concrete sleepers from its base.

With the buffer-stop now successfully loaded, the train set off for Inch while at the same time the excavator on its low-loader headed for Inch by road, where it was to undertake the unloading. First off was the buffer stop, which was placed by the excavator in its final position at the end of the headshunt. The unloading of the turnout components and the setting out in their correct position on the timbers went like clockwork, resulting in the job being finished by mid-afternoon leaving only the task of screwing down the chairs to complete the turnout. This success was due to the enthusiasm of the excavator owner, John Casement, as well as our very competent team.

We were lucky that in all of this heavy work the only casualty was myself, when a small accident resulted in a broken bone in my foot. It occurred during an unloading operation, a big disappointment, as it meant that I could not continue with the remainder of the work as I had planned. One small consolation was the knowledge that the project was now effectively finished as far as the IFI grant was concerned. All that remained was the laying of track to the bay platform, which I knew would be straightforward and capable of being completed by our experienced permanent way team.

*Above*: The Sleeper gantry in action, manned by John Henry, Barney Graham, Dessie Morrison and Andy Cook.
*Author*

*Below*: Ballasting the Inch Abbey line on 13 May 2006.
*Wilson Adams*

Thus, my involvement in permanent way and construction work ended much sooner than I had expected. I had greatly enjoyed the challenge and had the satisfaction of feeling that something worthwhile had been achieved. Various day-by-day experiences had built up a warm camaraderie between myself and an enthusiastic team of volunteers who are to be congratulated and should be proud of what they have accomplished under the most primitive working conditions.

I also knew I was going to miss the memorable experience of travelling back to base in the brake-van at the end of a hard day's work. It was always a joy to stand in the open balcony of the train watching the landscape pass by at about 20 mph, thus allowing time to appreciate the unspoilt scenery, scents of wild flowers and perhaps watch a pair of buzzards wheeling in the sky above.

**Footnotes**

1   Gerry Cochrane, Barney Graham, Dessie Morrison, Phil McGivern (JCB), David Trotter.

2   John Henry, George Legg, George Walker and Andy Cook.

***Left***: The buffer stop is unloaded, with Andy Cook and George Walker on the wagon.

***Left***: Inch Abbey station in use. RPSI 0-6-0ST *RH Smyth* in action on St Patrick's Day 2006.

*Norman Johnston*

# CHAPTER 8

# MONEY FOR OLD RAILS

The easy part of establishing any railway preservation project is formulating the idea but little can be achieved without finance. I learned this lesson very quickly during 1983 which was a period of activity mainly of an administrative and communications nature. The costs of stamps, stationary, telephone charges and photographic promotion were a drain on my private finances but thankfully, this situation was soon recognised by an early supporter, Bill Gillespie, who generously contributed to the escalating costs as the months went by, a gesture very much appreciated.

Progress was rapid during the next few years, only to be matched by the escalating costs of getting the scheme off the ground. Funding, or lack of it, was the main obstacle and worry which was to constantly dog this project throughout its history.

There was great urgency during 1984 to get Phase One started in order to let potential supporters, particularly DDC, see that this was a serious undertaking and not 'pie in the sky'.

The donation of land by Lord Dunleath was the first significant event at this time, which helped enormously. This vote of confidence on his part gave us courage to approach the local business community for a little financial help, an activity which I found difficult but which seemed to come naturally to David Trotter.

I vividly remember the two of us visiting various shops in Downpatrick and explaining to the owners all the advantages for the local economy and particularly for themselves whenever the scheme was up and running.

Point blank refusals were embarrassing but the pain was relieved by the one positive reaction that day from Tom Gibney, owner of the local paint shop.

By the summer of that year, the financial situation became more urgent with the sudden opportunity of acquiring the body of the BCDR Royal Saloon. The dilemma we faced was that we could not ignore such a prize exhibit but initial negotiations revealed that the carriage was within weeks of being cut up for firewood. The final cost agreed was £35 (firewood value) and, with the goodwill of Walter Watson, the British army, the RAF at Bishopscourt and favourable rates from Beattie Crane Hire we were able, with a little help from our supporters, to acquire this most historic exhibit. At this stage the only finance we had was that provided by our shareholders and generous supporters which amounted to about £600.

This saw the beginning of a frenetic period of acquisitions which was to last for the next five years and which was to have serious financial consequences for many years thereafter.

As the months went by, the lack of finance was the main topic of discussion at meetings, and in general conversation, with various ideas being considered. A steady trickle of donations had been coming in but nothing sufficient to meet our expected needs.

One idea which we explored was the request for sponsoring a 'yard of track' in America. Requests for publicity for this promotion were sent to the *Irish Echo* and *Irish World*. An excellent article describing our scheme appeared in *Ireland Digest*, offering a yard of track for a donation of $50 and although this was unsuccessful (we got two donations) it did lead to a surprising and lucrative result from an unexpected quarter some time later (see *Buy a Yard of Irish Track*).

Our first major breakthrough was a grant of £1,500 received from The Pilgrim Trust for preliminary restoration work on the Royal Saloon which was a great morale booster and very timely. This grant was followed three years later by a further grant of £2,305.

Another possible source of financial assistance we

considered was the National Heritage Memorial Fund. Their local representative at that time, Mr Charles Kinaghan, was invited to Downpatrick and given a tour of inspection of our museum by our Chairman, Robert Edwards and myself, a visit sharply etched in my memory as a result of an incident that could have had a dramatic ending, and one that would not have been to the benefit of our scheme.

After touring the Downpatrick end of our development it was decided to inspect the western end, entering via the abandoned Ardglass branch from the busy Ballydugan Road.

Robert's Landrover was ideal for this purpose, as this part of the original track bed had a very rough surface and was much overgrown since the closure of the railway. We continued to drive in the direction of the Loop Platform, leaving a gate open, as there was no sign of any farm stock around and we were aware that we would return shortly.

On our return journey however, a herd of cows had materialised from nowhere and were massed on the track bed between us and the open gate. Robert stopped his Landrover well short in order not to panic the animals. We realised it would be necessary for one of us to try to get behind the animals and drive them back. I drew the short straw – Well, we couldn't ask our guest to chase cows through the muck and Robert was driving. But, as everyone knows, cows have minds of their own and they took off at a gallop through the open gate, before I could cut them off. I was now hoping that they would continue along the main line and not take the Ardglass branch, as there was nothing to stop them stampeding out on to the busy Ballydugan Road. But, as if the points were set for the Ardglass branch, they naturally headed in that direction. I had to head them off, which I eventually succeeded in doing, just before the exit on to the main road and then I had to drive them all the way back. During this period, which probably took the best part of an hour, my companions, who had been sitting yarning in the comfort of the Landrover, had the nerve to ask what had kept me! Sadly, after all this effort and my grand display of rounding up cattle, it was all to no avail, as our request for funding was unsuccessful.

## Eastern promise

The failure of the London businessman to provide funds for the transport costs of the Brazil locomotives, referred to in Chapter 4, was to lead directly to our first big financial breakthrough. The Industrial Development Board (IDB) became aware of the difficulty we had experienced with the shipping agent and, knowing that we were trying to raise funds from the promotion of a 'yard of track,' they decided to include an article on our track promotion in their 'house' magazine, which was intended for circulation in Japan.

The article caught the imagination of the Public Relations firm Burson-Marsteller in Tokyo, who kindly promoted our scheme in the leading Tokyo newspaper, the *Asahi Evening News*, with a circulation of 12 million. They ran the following article:-

### Buy a Yard of Irish Track

*There is a call for cooperation from Northern Ireland to 'buy a yard of track'.*

*A railway line 14 kilometres long between the capital of County Down and a port town on the sea was abolished 35 years ago. Construction has already started on a plan to revive the line and run trains over it. Part of the line is scheduled to open for service in the summer of 1986. A steam locomotive will pull a 19th century royal coach along the line.*

*If you pay 8,000 yen you can own one yard of track. The name and address of the person who purchases a yard will be carved in Japanese in the actual ties, and a photograph of the imprinted ties and a certificate will be sent to the buyer. About 100 people have already made inquiries at the company which introduced this plan to Japan.*

*One couple applied to buy a yard saying they would like to go together some day to the actual site. They now have a wonderful dream. A young mother said "It's for the sake of my two year old daughter". She added in an excited voice, "We are now living in an apartment, so we probably will move eventually. Please carve the nostalgic address of the place where my husband stayed when he was studying in Portugal."*

*In the United States where there are many descendants of immigrants from Ireland, there has been great cooperation from people wanting to buy land in their homeland, in connection with the plan to revive the railway.*

*In various parts of Britain you find what are called preservation railways. Those who like railroads contribute money to buy track and locomotives and run trains at weekends carrying tourists. People in various occupations, including university professors, lawyers and postmen come with their own lunches to oil the locomotives and shovel coal.*

**Above:** Observed by Bob Edwards and the author, the Tokyo Broadcasting System team film the railway.

**Above:** Mrs Tsoyako Yasomitsu and the author, photographed by Mr Yasomitsu at the Loop Platform.

*They are adults who like playing with trains more than anything else.*

*In Japan today deficit local JNR lines and private railways in outlying areas are being abolished one after the other. Locomotives and coaches which are no longer needed are taken apart. Parts such as number plates and headlamps sell like hot cakes at exhibit sales, but the remains are turned into scrap.*

*Even if the collections of individuals increase, railways will not be resurrected.*

In addition, Burson-Marsteller set up a stall promoting our 'yard of track' offer at an exhibition organised by a large department store in Tokyo. In return for a donation of 8,000 Yen, each donor would receive a certificate, a personal brass name plate attached to his yard of track with a photograph to prove it.

The effect of all this publicity was overwhelming and, at times, quite embarrassing. On one occasion before we had even laid a yard of track, a film team from Tokyo Broadcasting System arrived on our site, hoping to film a working railway. However, they were very impressed with what they saw of the remains of the original railway and could see the potential in our proposals for its restoration.

They promised a return visit whenever we had made some progress.

Some weeks later, my embarrassment was further compounded when I received a very elaborate and colourful tourist promotion brochure from Japan which promoted our railway, which was shown rubbing shoulders with Big Ben and the 'Changing of the Guard' at Buckingham Palace.

Needless to say, I didn't complain, after being asked to meet a representative of the IDB's Japanese department in Belfast for what I thought would be a discussion on my method of inscribing over four hundred brass plates with Japanese inscriptions. To my astonishment, I was informed that we were on our way to the bank, where I received a cheque for over £5,000 with an expectation of more to follow. This was a very timely and vital injection of finance which, without doubt, made the difference between success and failure of our scheme.

True to their earlier promise, by mid-summer the Japanese returned again with their TV cameras to make a film for Japanese Television. This time we had the track laid to within 100 yards of the Loop Platform although our only motive power was a plate-layers trolley, (a board with four wheels). They were able to photograph some of the brass donation plates which had hastily been fixed to the track some 24 hours earlier.

The Guinness steam locomotive, now housed in our new shed, although not operational, was of great interest but they were more interested in the Royal Saloon carriage. They were aware of this historic exhibit and insisted on filming it even when I explained that it wasn't on our site and was in very poor condition. In fact, most sane-minded people would have considered it to be an absolute wreck. The problem was compounded by the fact that the carriage was in a high security location at Bishopscourt RAF airfield.

**Above:** Tokyo Broadcasting System at Bishopscourt, filming our glorious Royal Saloon.

It didn't help matters that in 1986 the 'troubles' were at their height and although some of us had security clearance (which took weeks to obtain) the six members of the Japanese film crew had not. After some hasty arrangements, access was eventually granted.

Now for the moment I was dreading, when the film crew came face to face with the once glorious Royal Saloon. I did warn them but language difficulties did not seem to adequately prepare them for the shock. After thirty years as a hen house and with most of its external panelling missing exposing most of its slender ribs, what else should they have expected? Their first reaction after recovering from the shock was to fall about laughing and making comments which I could not understand. Probably just as well.

I think, to save face, they went through the motions of filming our 'prize exhibit' in quite a lot of detail. Perhaps, after all, they could see the potential that we all took for granted.

They did manage to produce an excellent film which was broadcast on Japanese television and which definitely put Downpatrick on the map.

The reaction of the Japanese people in general was very supportive and from time to time over the last 20 years we have had visits from some of the donors who have come to see their nameplate on the track. In addition, over the years, I receive letters and Christmas cards from some of our new friends in Japan.

We were all most grateful for this support from Japan which was instrumental in getting our project under way.

## Earning our keep

December 1987 was another significant date which marked the beginning of our revenue earning operations with Santa Trains operating to the Loop Platform during the three weekends preceding Christmas. Special services were introduced also on St Patrick's Day, the Easter weekend, weekends in July and August and ending the season with Ghost Trains at Halloween. Special school days were also introduced which proved very popular with children and teachers. In addition to train rides at most events, we also provided light refreshments for our visitors.

All this effort by our volunteers was producing much needed revenue but the financial benefit appeared to be gobbled up by our insurance company. Up until this period, the premium had been reasonable but once the trains began to operate, premiums rocketed.

Insurance cover was required for public liability, steam boilers, steam engines, air vessels, and volunteers' personal accident cover. All this was essential as we could not operate without it.

We could not afford to insure other areas, such as building contents or our exhibits, such as carriages. Fortunately, the insurance of the buildings was the responsibility of DDC which was to be of great importance later.

With a steam locomotive now on site, our main priority was to find sufficient funding for its restoration. This

*Above:* RPSI 0-4-0ST *Guinness* in action on 17 March 1993. With Down Cathedral rising above the exhaust, the approaching train is seen from the Loop Platform.

*Norman Johnston*

locomotive, bearing the familiar name of *Guinness*, was on long-term lease from the RPSI at a rental of £200 per year, so the sooner we had it earning its keep, the better.

Costs associated with this project were considerable because, in addition to the annual rent, there was the matter of insurance costs and hefty restoration expenditure, even allowing for the fact that all the work would be carried out by our volunteers. The RPSI also required us to obtain a bank bond of £5,000 for the duration of the rent period, the cost of which would normally have been £250. In this instance our own bank, the First Trust in Downpatrick, generously waived the charge, surely a move that proves that banks have a heart after all!

As this locomotive was originally built for Guinness's Brewery in Dublin, we presumed that this firm would have some interest in our scheme, so we invited their promotions team to visit Downpatrick in the hope of obtaining sponsorship. We pulled out all the stops, gave them a detailed tour of inspection, outline of our future plans and offered to display their own product. We had high expectations, given that our locomotive carried their name in large, brass lettering. However, our timing was unfortunate as a protracted strike at their brewery delayed their decision which, when it eventually came, was negative.

Indeed, it was very difficult to get any sponsorship for this project and the scores of organisations we contacted

throughout Ireland and further afield, did not appear to share our enthusiasm for steam locomotives. Those contacted during this period included the Ireland Fund, Trust House Forte, Ford Motor Co, Rural Community Projects Awards, Community Arts Awards, and Paul Getty Trust, all to no avail.

At this time many ideas were being considered for the production of additional funds, with even a traditional ballot resulting in a welcome £420.

## Grant-assisted projects

In 1986 a special fund, the International Fund for Ireland (IFI), was set up as a result of the Anglo-Irish Agreement by the Irish and British governments, which stated that the two governments would co-operate to promote the economic and social development of those parts of Ireland which had suffered most severely from the consequences of instability and to consider the possibility of securing international support for this work. The contributors were the United States, Canada and New Zealand.

We felt that our scheme satisfied the objectives of the fund and in early 1988 we received a vote of confidence from the NITB, acting as agents for the IFI. The result was the approval of a grant of £15,000, which represented 50% of the cost of the restoration of the Guinness locomotive, together with the purchase of CIÉ carriages Nos 1918, 2419 & 3223.

A £1,000 grant was received from the Enkalon Foundation, whilst the First Trust Bank provided a grant of £300 to assist with the restoration of our first vintage carriage, GS&WR No 836.

The year 1987 was shaping up to be the most hectic of all. Not only were we in the middle of major acquisitions but I was also under pressure to produce designs for the station building and workshop, for which we were hoping to get financial assistance from the European Community.

This EEC grant plan was a cross-border tourist scheme for the border counties. There was some doubt initially as to whether County Down would be eligible so it was a great relief when we received confirmation that it was.

Grants were subsequently approved, with the European Regional Development Fund providing 50%. The Northern Ireland Tourist Board promised 25% and Down District Council agreed to provide the remaining 25%.

The project was to be administered by DDC who appointed the Design Team. I was accepted as architect on a voluntary basis (forgoing my fees) as contribution in kind.

The approved costs were, workshop £58,900, station building £68,800, and track materials £43,000.

By the autumn of 1987, I had received all the necessary approvals and had submitted drawings with cost estimates for the construction of the station building and workshop to DDC, for their approval to proceed to tender stage. Knowing that the overall estimates had to be what the Council regarded as reasonable, I had made sure that there were no unnecessary frills. Even heating had been omitted from the workshop.

I had pointed out that the costs should be regarded as the absolute minimum necessary to provide the basic accommodation required and, as well as that, allowance should also be made for the deep foundation expected for the station building.

When the tenders were received, DDC demanded more cuts which resulted in the omission of roof insulation in the workshop, together with cuts in the electrical power and lighting installations. In the station building, wall plastering had to be omitted and severe reductions in the electrical installation had also to be made.

One unfortunate consequence of the omission of the roof insulation in the workshop is that, in certain weather conditions, condensation dripping from the roof gives the impression that it is raining and makes for uncomfortable working conditions.

Although at the outset I had volunteered to provide my architectural services as a contribution in kind, at the conclusion of the contract I was informed by the NITB that they had factored in professional fees which would be in addition to the approved cost. The ERDF and the NITB would provide 75% which would leave DDC to come up with the remaining 25%, which they had not allowed for.

I made the proposal to DDC that I would donate my total fees to the Railway Company if they would agree to fund the remaining 25%. After some hesitation and cajoling this was agreed and the Company benefited to the value of approximately £10,000 which included the Council's £2,500 contribution. Most of this unexpected windfall helped to fund the restoration of our first vintage carriage, while the remainder went towards general expenses.

## The bigger picture

In order to promote tourism in the District, DDC appointed a firm of consultants[1] to recommend suitable candidates for tourist development in their area. The Directors of the Railway Museum had also being considering future development, as the full potential of our scheme could not be achieved with our present limited track and lack of a meaningful destination.

As mentioned in Chapter 2, the original intention to extend the railway to Ardglass was being frustrated by the non co-operation of some landowners, so we decided on the more achievable options, namely to extend the line westward to Ballydugan Corn Mill and northward to Inch Abbey.

This was going to be our most challenging and important capital development to date, which would be planned in three stages as described in detail in Chapter 5.

The proposal was supported and encouraged by the NITB, as well as the consultants advising DDC, and suggested that the scheme had the potential to attract 100,000 visitors annually when fully completed.

On the strength of this advice and our own assessment, we appointed a local firm of consulting engineers to prepare a feasibility study with costs for the three stages.

The estimated cost including fees was £398,800, a massive figure by any standards, necessitating a very careful and thorough grant application.

In March 1992 a detailed submission, including a business plan, was submitted to the IFI for 90% of the cost; the remaining 10% was expected to be provided by DDC. The railway's contribution was estimated to be £105,000 in voluntary labour.

By July we had an offer of grant from the IFI for all three stages, as requested, which cleared the way for an immediate start on Stage One.

This stage proceeded without any major hitches but Stage Two to Ballydugan was proving tricky, due to the difficulty of obtaining agreement from the landowner. As discussions looked like becoming protracted, it was decided to divert our attention to the Inch Abbey extension for which, by this stage, we had acquired the landowner's agreement in principle.

By this time, six years had elapsed since the grant had been approved. The excessive delay, detailed in Chapter 7, had a serious effect on the value of our grant, which was diminishing by the day as we did not benefit from any interest.

The estimated cost of this stage was £140,000 but the nine tenders received ranged from £252,000 to £348,000, massively over our budget, which necessitated a complete reappraisal of our options. Drastic action was required if we wanted the project to proceed. After much discussion with our Consultants, the only solution that I could see was for the volunteers to now undertake most of the work and for a contractor to carry out the highly specialised bridge construction as described in detail in Chapter 7.

This was agreed and by January 1999 the bridge was finished leaving us with barely sufficient funds to complete the remaining track and platform at Inch Abbey. It was to take a further five years for the volunteers to complete their share of the work, the last few years being very stressful as the NITB were, understandably, getting impatient with the delay and finally issuing an ultimatum threatening to withdraw our grant. It was now over ten years since the grant had been awarded. However, with a final push and major effort, as detailed in Chapter 7, the Inch Abbey extension opened for business in September 2004.

## Great Expectations

During the long saga of the preceding project, the Directors identified three priority projects which were regarded as essential for the logical development of our scheme. These were:

1 Restoration of our two steam locomotives.
2 The provision of a permanent locomotive shed.
3 The building of a carriage display gallery.

Finding the funding would of course be the big challenge. By good fortune, the National Lottery Heritage Fund had recently been set up. Its main function was the protection of heritage and our scheme fitted all their criteria. Other potential candidates for funding were the ERDF and of course, DDC.

We were fortunate at this stage to be joined on our committee by Dr Austin Smyth, Professor of Transport at the New University of Ulster (NUU) who took on the position of Marketing Officer. In addition, he volunteered to prepare a business plan for the grant applications I was struggling with at that time.

**The estimated costs of the three projects were:-**

| | | |
|---|---|---|
| 1 | Restoration of locomotives | £75,000 |
| 2 | Locomotive shed | £155,000 |
| 3 | Carriage gallery | £269,350 |

## Project 1  Restoration of the steam locomotives

By early 1996, grants totalling £75,000 (the estimated cost) had been secured from the HLF and ERDF for the restoration of our Orenstein & Koppel steam locomotive No 3, together with the restoration of the boiler for sister locomotive No 1, both undergoing restoration at Downpatrick.

Locomotive No 3 was sent to the RPSI at Whitehead for a complete overhaul, while work to the boilers was undertaken by Woolf Engineering of Ballymena. One boiler was found to be repairable but the other was considered to be beyond restoration, resulting in a new build being required.

Although the completion of this project was very protracted, and resulted in a crippling cost overrun of £25,000, locomotive No 3 has been a big success. However, the financial consequences, although eased by a further contribution from the HLF, were to plague us during the following few years.

## Project 2  Locomotive shed

At an early stage in this development, an opportunity arose for the acquisition of a railway goods shed at Maghera station on the former Derry Central Railway, as described in detail in Chapter six.

In common with all our great opportunities, there was a major problem – finance. The cost of moving this large stone building was estimated at £2,500, which of course we did not have. To add to our difficulties, the building was due for demolition within weeks. Pressure had returned with a vengeance.

Exhaustive efforts to fund this project were unsuccessful until the eleventh hour, when the Downpatrick Project Board provided a grant of £2,000, mainly due to the efforts of Jack McIlheron, a councillor with DDC.

Obtaining grants, in fact, proved to be the easy part. However, the following two years is a period I would prefer to forget.

The trouble began when we were informed at very short notice that DDC had approved their share of the grant and that a minimum of £14,000 and preferably £28,000 had to be spent before the end of their financial year. This gave the architect approximately three months to obtain Building Control and Planning approvals, finalise contract documents and obtain competitive tenders – an impossible task.

This was a serious situation. If we lost this amount of grant it would not be possible to proceed with the scheme.

So the only answer was to split the project into two. The first contract would be for the piling and floor slab. It would be possible to complete this section in time to meet the District Council's spending targets. Contract No 2 would comprise the superstructure and completion. The risk with this approach was that we would be committed to the full project before we were sure of the overall cost.

The first contract went according to plan, leaving £100,000 for the completion of the project. By August 1997 tenders were received, the lowest being £178,600. This left us with a whopping shortfall of £79,000.

Cuts to achieve this scale of savings were impossible without compromising important aspects of the project. Some of the main cuts proposed were omitting the station canopy, a feature window, external stonework, mechanical and electrical installation and a reduction in the quality of the perimeter fence.

These changes would have resulted in a building that bore little resemblance to the original, which we regarded as an exhibit in its own right. Needless to say, I resisted most of these changes and appealed to our three sponsors to provide the additional funds necessary.

Where possible, voluntary labour was offered in order to augment this by undertaking the painting and additional electrical work. The shortfall was eventually reduced to £36,000, achieved without compromising the original character of the building. We were fortunate that the HLF took a sympathetic view and this enabled the contract to be completed in reasonable time.

This whole debacle, however, had an unfortunate consequence for our reputation with the HLF and it resulted in their rejection of our application for the restoration of the Royal Saloon which had been under consideration at that time.

The only consolation for all the pain was that the locomotive shed (Maghera Shed) has now been completed in close resemblance to the original. The fact that we have acquired a canopy for our station, which gave rise to this whole project, is a feature which gives great satisfaction to us all.

## Project 3  Carriage display gallery

Our collection of unique vintage carriages had grown to such an extent that it was necessary to provide suitable accommodation for them. This was critical as it was no longer acceptable to store restored carriages outside, to be subjected to the weather as well as vandalism. Carriages awaiting restoration were also vulnerable as it became a continuous struggle to keep them covered during winter storms.

With part of the funding already promised from the ERDF for this project, the final outstanding grant was expected from the HLF. A detailed submission had been made which passed the first stage and subsequent discussions with HLF in England gave rise to optimism.

However, it was during this period that a local committee of the HLF was set up in Northern Ireland and their decision to reject our application was a disappointment which put at risk our unique vintage carriage collection and virtually put a stop to our vintage carriage restoration programme.

As a direct result of this decision, we had to forfeit a grant of £65,000 which had been promised from the ERDF as there was no chance of the project proceeding within the planned time scale. Thus ended our capital developments for the foreseeable future.

In 2008 a less ambitious application was submitted to the HLF by Philip McKinstery. Expectations are high that this will now receive the consideration it deserves.

## Financial stress

By early 1990 the results of the previous three years of intense activity, particularly with regard to the acquisition of large exhibits such as carriages and locomotives, had left us with a considerable overdraft and with little prospect of being able to reduce it. In fact, this trend was to continue with a steady increase for the next ten years to the point where we were close to becoming insolvent.

It was a very difficult time, particularly for our Treasurer,

Alan Major, because although we all appreciated the seriousness of the situation, we found it very difficult to get the finances under control. These problems eventually prompted various methods of improving our financial position. One generous offer from a fellow Director pledged £5,000 if we could match this through a major fund-raising campaign. Alas, this also failed due to inertia and fatigue.

Severe warnings by some of our distinguished Directors about the consequences of our lack of professionalism eventually had an impact.

By early 1996 our overdraft had risen to an unacceptable level, forcing the Directors to invite the shareholders to lend £100 each, to offset the overdraft in the short term. In the longer term, a serious attempt to place the Company's finances on a more business-like footing was discussed and approved by our Bank. This resulted in a moratorium on all expenditure, a move which led to severe frustration among our volunteers, who found themselves unable to proceed with their various projects. The situation regarding capital works was different as no development would be approved without 100% grant aid – at least that was the theory, but cost over-runs continued to impact negatively on our overall financial situation.

## Sink or Swim

During the sixteen years or so in which Alan Major held the honorary post of Treasurer, he preformed this thankless task, in extremely difficult financial circumstances, with great enthusiasm and dedication. However, the scale of the job by the year 2001 bore no resemblance to the operations of those early years and it was obvious that professional help had become essential.

Deliverance came when John Beaumont, with a background in professional banking and long experience in railway preservation with the RPSI, agreed to act as our honorary financial advisor. After examining the overall financial situation, he confirmed that the situation was not good – but there was a way forward.

What he found was a crippling loan, major overheads, heavy insurance premiums and a large bank overdraft. These, together with the absence of overall financial planning and budgetary control, were responsible for expenditure exceeding income with the inevitable result.

A stark decision had to be made to pay off staff, combined with obtaining an injection of outside funding as a matter of extreme urgency. The moratorium on expenditure still held and was to be adhered to strictly.

Consequently, a sub-committee[2] was set up to prepare and make a presentation to DDC, which eventually resulted in a cash injection to get us over the short term problems and allow the completion of the Inch extension.

With John's hands-on approach, and with the assistance of Patricia McGrath, our part-time book-keeper, this new regime transformed our financial position beyond all recognition, giving us all confidence in the future viability of our railway. It was a classic example of the value of getting early professional financial advice.

**Footnotes**

1   McKay Report.
2   Councillor J McIlheron, J Beaumont, M Collins & G Cochrane.

CHAPTER 9
# BEWARE OF TRAINS

The movement of trains, and the transition from a static situation into a real operating railway, was a significant event which began early in 1987 when our E class Maybach diesel locomotive became available to carry out useful work.

It was now time to organise a training programme for those members who wished to become drivers, firemen/women and steam raisers and our Chairman, Robert Edwards, with his many years of experience in the RPSI, lost no time in setting this up.

Safety was very much in our minds of course, and a special effort was made to instil this into the minds of all operating staff. Train operations present situations which have the highest potential for injury to both staff and visitors. Even with a limited train operating speed of 25 miles per hour, serious accidents were possible.

Colin Holliday was appointed Locomotive Inspector and undertook to implement the training scheme, which resulted in the introduction of a rule book, incident report forms, a signing-on book for operating staff and an agreement to operate on a 'one engine in steam' principle, (even though we

*Right:* History was made on 10 October 1987, when loco 421 hauled the first train to arrive at the Loop platform.
From left to right are: Vincent Gardiner, Darren Rodgers, Albert Sage, Des Sage, Conor Sage, Kenneth Beattie, Michael Gardiner, Peter King, John Hughes, David Trotter (driving) and the author.

*Edward Duly*

had only diesels) until a safe signalling system was introduced. Detailed arrangements were agreed for the safe operation of public train services but it was not uncommon among our volunteers for the new situation to give rise to occasional disputes over the interpretation of the rules. This was also the case in regard to Works trains when the Permanent Way Department had full possession of the track.

By Easter, we had our first major publicity opportunity in the form of a visit from Ulster Television. Needless to say, David Trotter was, as usual, in his element, driving our restored Maybach locomotive up and down the track while UTV's Pamela Gardner interviewed him on camera. This publicity by Ulster Television was followed by a visit from members of the Irish Transport Trust bringing with them a large fleet of vintage buses.

We were now being taken seriously by people, some of whom had earlier thought we were just 'playing trains' and had not been slow to tell us so.

Locomotive E421 was very much David's baby and, having nursed it back to life, he was very reluctant to let anyone else drive it. No work could be undertaken until David, as driver, checked in.

This was the first example of the disadvantage of depending on one person to carry out a key function and which was to be repeated many times in the succeeding years. During my period as General Manager I should, with hindsight, have ensured that our volunteers were trained to undertake as many tasks as their ability allowed.

As GM, I was not aware that other volunteers were equally keen to drive the 'E' and that a mutinous situation was developing. It took a deputation of volunteers to alert me to the problem, which was eventually resolved by an injection of common sense and the setting up of a driver instruction course.

## "Change for Ballynoe, Killough and Ardglass"

This was the call which resonated around the roof of the Loop Platform many times a day from 1892 and was last heard in January 1950. The occasion was the arrival of the main line train from Belfast or Newcastle when the guard announced that passengers should change for the branch line train if they were going to Downpatrick or Ardglass. Therefore, it was a very historic event when the next train that pulled into the Loop Platform did so on Saturday 10 October 1987.

We had been working very hard all that day, trying to get the last 60 foot panel of track laid to the Loop Platform. The enthusiasm of our track gang was such that it was nearly dark by the time we had gathered up all our equipment and returned to the depot. But the day was not over yet. After some preparation for night running, we all piled into the cab of the locomotive and David drove back to the Loop, where we all alighted on the platform with the guard shouting, "Change for Ballynoe, Killough and Ardglass!"

This event was officially re-staged the following Saturday for all our members, only this time with our open wagon and brake van. Great preparations had been made to mark the occasion. A table had been erected in the open wagon, was laid out with plenty of food and drink, and a small celebratory party at the Loop was enjoyed by all. Unfortunately, the down side was that I do not recollect any work being carried out that day!

Our first formal train operation was a VIP trip in November 1987 to the Loop Platform, a location which

was planned to become the focal point of all our public operations and the central point in our railway system linking Ballydugan, Inch Abbey and Downpatrick.

The platform, big enough to accommodate large crowds, has an overall roof and two platform faces, one serving the main line and the other serving Downpatrick. The only drawback was that it was very exposed, remote and only accessible by railway. One of its main attractions is its timelessness and isolation with no evidence of any modern development for miles in any direction.

Taking part on this trip were over eighty members and partners from the two most important organisations in the town, Down District Council and Downpatrick Chamber of Trade. Our guests piled into the only operational vehicle we had, the recently acquired 25 ton NCC brake van with its open balcony at each end and central cabin.

For many, this was their first time on a train, while for older people, alighting on the Loop Platform brought back memories of former days when the railway played such an important part in the life of the town. Our guests were treated to refreshments dispensed from our brown van. This was a four-wheel, covered van with sliding side doors. However, the guests had to enjoy their refreshments 'on the hoof' on the platform. No such luxuries as a dining saloon were available to us at that time.

One incident that occurred, and which I will never forget, happened seconds before the train pulled out of our temporary station in Downpatrick. I was standing filming at track level on the opposite side of the train when I noticed in my viewfinder, a VIP on the ground, crawling between the wheels under the brake van! Apparently, someone had dropped something and he was in the act of retrieving it. Thinking about the incident now chills me, as our grand event could have been as famous as the opening of the Liverpool and Manchester Railway in 1830, when William Huskisson, MP for Liverpool, was killed by the first train.

I refrain from naming the gentleman involved, to save any embarrassment, except to say that this incident could have left Downpatrick seriously lacking in items of hardware!

## Popular events

With the first successful public event behind us, and at the bottom of a steep learning curve, we felt confident enough to advertise *Santa Train Rides* for the following month, December 1987. Jim Perry purchased presents and arranged a present wrapping session in his home with the assistance of his late wife, Mary, as well as volunteers Albert Sage and his sons.

Again, passengers would be carried in the brake van

while Santa was in his grotto in the brown van at the Loop. On the three Saturdays before Christmas, over 500 passengers were carried, a staggering figure, given that the accommodation was limited to one brake van.

The event was our first big success financially, producing £650 over the three days. We felt rich! The only anxiety during the event was the possibility of running out of presents but this was narrowly averted by Jim's excellent organisational skills.

The following Christmas (December 1988), the season opened with Santa arriving by train at our new temporary platform in Downpatrick, to be greeted by hoards of parents and excited children accompanied by a fire engine, which conveyed Santa to the centre of the town where he performed the switching-on ceremony of the Christmas lights.

Santa[1] Train Rides have been a popular feature of our operations every year since and we are now getting parents returning with their children, having visited us as children themselves.

To-day, with our much improved facilities such as comfortable carriages, steam operation, dining saloon, dual grottos, station facilities and model railway layout, the 'Santa Experience' has become our most popular and lucrative event.

St Patrick's Day, Easter, May Day and Halloween are all special occasions at our railway, while the summer weekends are also very popular.

Early in our first year of operations we were getting requests from primary schools in Down District, and the greater Belfast area, to provide facilities for school visits. This idea appealed to us and arrangements were made for two days in June to be set aside for its purpose.

We expected to have one of our 'new' ex CIÉ carriages, No 1918, ready for this occasion. Although this carriage was a far cry from our 'Edwardian Experience' ambitions, it would be a major improvement on the brake van and, as it had tables, it would also allow children the facility of refreshments at their seats. One local school, Holy Family, Teconnaught, asked if we could arrange to have tickets punched by the guard on the train. This was an unforeseen problem, as at this stage we had no printed tickets, but we were as enthusiastic as the school kids and agreed to pull out all the stops. Tickets were produced manually with the aid of a specially made rubber stamp, coloured card and a pair of scissors. This same school was so enthusiastic that they all turned up in Edwardian dress, children as well as staff, which added to the flavour of such a happy occasion.

These school visits made us realise that we could do much more, without incurring great expense, to improve our image by concentrating on minor, but important, details such as uniforms for 'front of house' staff. Not only would this improve our image and present a more

*Left:* Christmas 1989 at the loop Platform.

*Below:* Christmas 2006 at Downpatrick Station.
*Wilson Adams*

professional impression but, from a visitors' point of view, would give them confidence that the organisation was safe and responsible. The possibility of obtaining obsolete uniforms from NIR, although a bit too modern in style was thought to be a good short-term solution, particularly as they were donated.

As well as uniforms, traditional Edmondson tickets would add greatly to the experience for many passengers.

In more recent times, the visitors' enjoyment has been greatly enhanced by the efforts of our Commercial Manager, George Legg, who travels on the train giving a very graphic commentary on all items of interest throughout the journey, of the railway and its history.

## Special events

In an effort to increase our revenue, we were continuously exploring new markets, some of which were very successful while some were not too popular with our volunteer staff. Private parties, where a train including the Dining Saloon could be hired for an afternoon or evenings, were to become regular events. These were sometimes for children's parties or social groups. Hen parties were definitely not encouraged as they tended to go on into the small hours and get out of hand. Folk groups were another category that were difficult to control and, with trains in motion, they were felt to be a risk too far.

The variety of possible events on our railway is virtually limitless, as illustrated by a special train late one spring evening. On this occasion, the Downpatrick and Listowel Linkage Group (Downpatrick is twinned with Listowel, Co Kerry) hired our crack express, consisting of three carriages, including our 1920s-style Dining Saloon, for 90 guests. The theme of the evening, which was known to the guests, 45 of whom came up from Listowel, was based very loosely on the novel, *Murder on the Orient Express*.

Guests had all come in period dress and were looking forward, perhaps with some anxiety, to a gourmet meal in carriages suitably decorated for the event. The reason for the anxiety was that they were all aware that a murder was imminent but had no idea who the murderer was or who among them was to play 'victim'.

Judging by the sound of high spirits and gaiety during the meal, the forthcoming drama had little effect and the evening went with a real swing.

The filming of a scene from the famous movie *The Quiet Man* was at the request of BBC Northern Ireland, who had requested the use of our railway facility for their contribution to the annual *Children in Need* production.

Standing in for the original cast were Eamonn Holmes as John Wayne, Victoria Smurfitt as the red-head Maureen O'Hara and Gerry Anderson as the jarvey, Barry Fitzgerald.

The main action took place on Downpatrick station platform with Eamonn roughly dragging Victoria out of the train, aided and abetted by a large group of passengers (extras) who were thronging the platform. A 'row' developed among these 'passengers' which deteriorated into a monumental scuffle which eventually led to the Station Master and the train Guard lying in a heap on the platform.

The 'passengers' had to make a donation to the *Children in Need* appeal to enable them to take part in the action. Notable among these 'passengers', and the one thought to have been the main cause of the trouble was Barney Graham, one of our most respected volunteers, acting completely out of character.

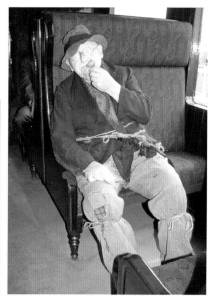

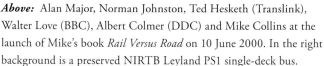

***Above:*** Alan Major, Norman Johnston, Ted Hesketh (Translink), Walter Love (BBC), Albert Colmer (DDC) and Mike Collins at the launch of Mike's book *Rail Versus Road* on 10 June 2000. In the right background is a preserved NIRTB Leyland PS1 single-deck bus.

One very memorable occasion was the visit of Sir Harry Secombe during the filming of a St Patrick's Day edition of ITV's popular programme *Highway*. This was in March 1991, when Sir Harry was well on in years but still as youthful as ever.

Over the years, our facilities have been used for productions by commercial film companies, who require some aspect of railway operation in their production. The most notable to date has been the film *Puckoon*, based on Spike Milligan's book of the same name. Although the film only achieved limited release, it resulted in a considerable boost to our revenue.

Small wedding receptions have also been accommodated with some success and there is tremendous potential for this type of event to be expanded, particularly as we now operate to Inch Abbey. I look forward to the time when we have the Royal Salon restored and can offer a 'Wedding Express' in Royal splendour. This would be unique to our railway, as no other organisation on the island of Ireland would have this capability.

There was a time when most small boys wanted to be an engine driver. Now that they have grown up, they have the opportunity on the DCDR to fulfil this ambition as among many of the attractions listed in our promotional material is the Footplate Experience Course. These courses give individual members of the public a chance of a 'hands-on' experience, by being actively involved for a day on the footplate, operating our steam locomotive. As evidence of his, or her, day on the footplate, our guest, who began the day in pristine overalls, is usually observed scrubbing furiously to remove the soot and grease from hands and face and usually goes home smelling of oil and steam.

## A Day in the Life of . . .

All these events make great demands on our volunteers who, despite everything, always respond with enthusiasm and professionalism no matter what the weather or time of day. It would probably come as a surprise to learn that on a normal operating day a minimum staff of 16 volunteers is necessary to ensure a safe and professional operation.

There are some fundamental differences between the operation of the original BCDR and our restored railway of to-day, the main one relating to the preparation of the steam locomotive for the day's duty. In former times there were cleaners, steam raisers, and shunters who prepared the locomotive, leaving it ready for the driver and fireman to drive off.

On our railway, all these duties are shared between the locomotive crew, which results in a very long and exhausting day. To give an idea of the labour involved, the following sequence of events is typical and begins with the driver or fireman opening up the premises about four hours before the event is due to begin. The steam locomotive has to be pulled out of the locomotive shed by a diesel shunter to allow the fire to be lit. The lighting of the fire is a ritual in itself, requiring skill and patience in arranging the firewood and coal. The aim is to avoid heating the boiler too quickly, since this can cause leaks due to expansion. The driver, by this time, would have inspected the locomotive both externally and internally, paying particular attention to the water level and making sure that the cylinder drain cocks were open. During the heating up period, coal would be loaded and the engine oiled, greased, cleaned and polished.

This is by no means a full description of the work involved in getting a steam engine ready at the start of the day and I haven't yet described the labour required at the end of the day! But it should be enough to illustrate why, on modern railways, the steam locomotive eventually gave way to diesels.

By the time the steam engine is ready, additional staff should have arrived and a complicated shunt of carriages is necessary to form the train for the day's event. The shunt is complicated due to the fact that we have very limited space available within our secure compound. Carriages not required for operations have to be shunted off the running lines to free up the platform, while the carriages required for that day's operation have to be retrieved from their various safe havens.

In addition to all this, a track inspection is necessary to make sure that no surprises are in store for the first train. Possible vandalism, fallen trees or broken rails are all distinct possibilities and it is usually the engine crew who carry out this important duty.

The Ticket Office staff are the first point of contact for the customers and it is essential that they are ready and well prepared when the doors open at the advertised time. This duty can be very stressful and it is important to have a cash float organised to avoid delay when the queues begin.

The Catering Department also plays an important role in the overall enjoyment of our visitors and is one that requires considerable preparation beforehand. Staff, by this time, have stocked up with fresh provisions and cleaned the carriage both inside and out, with particular attention being paid to the windows.

Our Dining Saloon is usually parked in the bay platform in Downpatrick but can also be located at Inch Abbey or the Loop Platform. On special occasions it can be included in the moving train, the role for which it was originally designed.

The Souvenir Shop, located in the station building,

would also by now have been cleaned and made ready for the first customers. This facility has recently been upgraded and transformed under the direction of George Legg, with the assistance of Herby Bodel. In addition to providing an additional point of interest for visitors, it plays a substantial role in providing additional revenue.

Of special interest to our younger visitors is the model railway layout, which was kindly donated by our Marketing Officer, Robert Gardiner. This extensive layout is presently located in our exhibition room at Downpatrick Station and supervised by Desmond Morrison. It was introduced to provide children with the opportunity of a 'hands-on' experience of operating model trains and to provide them with an interest while waiting to board the full-size train.

This layout still brings back memories of my first visit to a Model Engineers exhibition so many years ago which sparked my interest in railway modelling. I would like to think that our museum could inspire coming generations of children to engage in this absorbing hobby.

At the end of the day, with the last passenger gone, the volunteers have still many hours work ahead of them.

The steam locomotive crew make sure that by the time the engine arrived at the shed the fire is low and they will fill the boiler. At this stage, they will open the cylinder drain cocks and drop the fire. Finally the fireman cleans out the smoke box and ash pan, a very dirty, hot and dusty job.

While this is taking place, a diesel locomotive will be shunting the carriages back to their original locations.

The Dining Saloon staff will also be busy carrying out a thorough clean, and all waste food is disposed of before the doors can be closed and the staff sign off.

This is just a glimpse of the myriad of tasks involved in the smooth running of any public operating day on our railway but, for our volunteers, it is a labour of love.

**Footnotes**

1   Santas:  Walter Burke, Denis Cahill, Niall Cochrane, Mike Collins, Dr David Irwin, George Legg, Jim Perry & Albert Sage.

**Left:** Ex-GS&WR '90 class' 0-6-0T No 90 running round at Inch Abbey on St Patrick's Day 2008.

*Norman Johnston*

**Below centre:** Ex-CIÉ Maybach 0-6-0 diesel No E421 at King Magnus Halt with a demonstration freight train on 14 October 2006.

*Wilson Adams*

**Below lower:** Ex-LP&HC 0-6-0ST No 3 *RH Smyth* at King Magnus Halt on 5 August 2006.

*Wilson Adams*

**Left:** 0-6-0ST No 3 *RH Smyth* prepares to leave Downpatrick on 9 April 2007.

**Centre left:** Not quite what it seems! O&K No 3 is actually engaged in a shunt on 12 April 2004.

**Above right:** A stirring departure from Downpatrick for O&K No 3 on St Patrick's Day 2002, with drain cocks open.

**Lower left:** With Down Cathedral overlooking the scene, *RH Smyth* leaves Downpatrick for inch Abbey on 25 August 2007.

*All on this page*
*Norman Johnston*

***Upper left:*** Ex-LP&HC 0-6-0ST No 3 *RH Smyth* at Inch Abbey station with a demonstration goods on 21 October 2006.

***Upper right:*** O&K 0-4-0T No 3 heading towards the Loop platform with a Charter for Hamilton Road Presbyterian Church, Bangor, on 27 May 2006.

***Lower:*** A superb photograph of O&K 0-4-0T No 3 crossing the Quoile bridge on its way from Inch Abbey on 16 April 2006.

*All on this page*
*Wilson Adams*

***Top left:*** Ex-LP&HC 0-6-0ST No 3 *RH Smyth* passes the North Junction en route from Inch Abbey on 10 September 2006.

***Top right:*** A ghostly figure greets passengers at the Loop platform at Hallow'een 2006.

*Both Wilson Adams*

***Above:***

O&K 0-4-0T No 3 chuffs past Downpatrick shed, with coach 836 leading, in May 2001.

*Drew Sucksmith*

***Right:*** A nice study of O&K 0-4-0T No 3 at Inch Abbey station, on 16 April 2006.

*Wilson Adams*

CHAPTER 10
# MUSEUM STATUS

From its inception, the intention of the project was to allow visitors to experience Edwardian railway travel and, in some measure, to take part in the on-going restoration and operation of the railway.

Instead of being confined inside a building, this museum comprises buildings, miles of track, trackside flora and fauna, bridges, signals, signal cabins and stations, together with steam locomotives, carriages and wagons as expressed in the following Mission Statement:-

## Mission Statement

*Our aim is to restore a section of the original Belfast & County Down Railway as a working railway museum as it was in the early years of the 20th century, thereby promoting an understanding and appreciation of our railway heritage and social conditions of the period.*

*This aim will be achieved by collecting, restoring, operating and maintaining appropriate examples of buildings, locomotives, carriages, wagons and other items of railway equipment.*

*In addition to making the collection available to the general public, the museum is aimed at the promotion of tourism and the economic regeneration of Down District.*

*To support our main aim, exhibits from other local railways will be included in order to allow comparison between the different railway companies. In addition, more modern examples of our railway heritage will be considered for their commercial potential.*

I was anxious to strive for high professional standards where possible, even though the Museum would be administered and operated on a voluntary basis. This is even more important today, due to competition from other educational and leisure facilities, where high standards of presentation and service are expected from a more discerning public.

By a happy coincidence, the Museums and Galleries Commission were undertaking a review of Museums and related services in Northern Ireland in 1983 and I received an invitation to meet the review team to explain my feasibility study and progress to date.

An extract from the findings of the working party is reproduced in Appendix 1.

## Northern Ireland Museums Council

The MGC Report was of major importance to our Museum, as it led to the establishment of the Northern Ireland Museums Council (NIMC), which was to play such an important role in the successful development of our own scheme.

Established in 1993 on the order of the Minister of Education, the NIMC was charged with assisting local museums to develop their standards of collections care and visitor services. The Council also assumed responsibility for the UK-wide Standards Scheme – Museum Registration (now called Museum Accreditation).

Over the next few months, preparations were made within our organisation to meet the application requirements, with reasonable anticipation of success for membership of the NIMC and it was a great relief to receive Associate Membership in July 1994.

This success was due to a large extent to the then Director of NIMC, Mr Aidan Walsh and his staff, who so kindly and patiently assisted me through the many detailed

stages. One requirement was the need for us to have access to a Curatorial Adviser and we were most fortunate that this important role was undertaken by Ms Lesley Simpson BA, of Down County Museum, who has given me every assistance over the years, especially with regard to grant applications. Her advice at Management Committee level was a valued contribution.

Another important requirement was that we obtained professional conservation advice. In this case, Mr Mark Kennedy of the UFTM kindly agreed to act as our Conservation Advisor.

The influence of the NIMC was to lead to a more professional standard in our aims and activities which, apart from improved visitor experience, allowed us access to grants[1] for the conservation and restoration of exhibits. This was of great importance to the development of our museum and one which we exploited to the full.

A special effort was made to maximise the potential of our limited exhibition space on the first floor of the station building. Display is limited to small items and to historic photographs of the BCDR which were taken a few years before closure. These photographs were taken by Eric Russell and copies were donated to our museum by the North West of England Railway Society. This collection is augmented by photographs from my own collection, illustrating the work of our volunteers during the first twenty years of development. By this time in our evolving history, I was acting as Honorary Curator, an activity which I thoroughly enjoyed.

## Museum status

The year 2002 was a major milestone, when we received full museum registration. On this occasion, the Director of the NIMC, Mr Chris Bailey, attended a special ceremony in the station to present the certificate to a very proud gathering of Directors and volunteers.

Full Registration demonstrates that the museum meets the minimum standards of museum operation and is recognised as an indicator of responsible management by many funding bodies.

In order to achieve this, it was necessary to bring our records up to date, listing and numbering all our exhibits, preparing an Acquisitions and Disposal Policy, together with procedures to duplicate our records and provide a fireproof safe.

A second review, to improve standards generally, has been under way for some years and our museum has recently

***Left:*** Chris Bailey hands over the Certificate of Museum Registration to the Chairman, with Walter Burke in attendance.

*Norman Johnston*

attained Museum Accreditation, in no small part due to the persistence and dedication of our current Honorary Curator, Neil Hamilton, with advice and assistance again from the staff of the NIMC.

## Restoration and maintenance

By far the most demanding activity in our organisation, apart from train operations, is that of restoration and maintenance. These are ongoing activities which will remain an important feature of our museum. We have found that visitors, particularly children, are fascinated to see our volunteers in the midst of working on the restoration of carriages and locomotives which have all the appearance of being total wrecks. Once restored, the carriages and locomotives are then put into service to allow visitors to experience the unique delight of travel in the Edwardian period, although regular maintenance thereafter is vital to ensure safety and reliability.

I recall an occasion, while giving a guided tour of our workshop, when a young girl of about ten years of age told me that she preferred our museum to Northern Ireland's most prestigious Transport Museum at Cultra, in County Down. Needless to say, I was amazed and asked for an explanation. She answered by telling me that she liked to see carriages being restored. This type of feedback from the public is often expressed and gives great encouragement to

our volunteers.

The on-site restoration of our locomotives is very limited, as major overhauls are undertaken by outside contractors, such as the Railway Preservation Society of Ireland or Woolf Engineering of Ballymena. They have the specialist expertise and equipment for such work.

Routine maintenance of carriages and locomotives is carried out by our volunteers[2,] virtually on a daily basis, and the time and energy expended makes heavy demands on our limited engineering staff, all of whom are volunteers.

At the present time, our main activity is the restoration of carriages and wagons and of particular interest to me is our valuable collection of vintage carriages from the Victorian and Edwardian era. In the period covered by this book, we have acquired a unique collection of nine carriages, two of which have been restored and are now in operation. These are BCDR bogie carriage No 148 and GS&WR bogie carriage No 836. Our third vintage carriage restoration, currently in progress, of BCDR Railmotor No 2, is expected to be completed in 2011.

The carriage collection has the potential to be the most historic and extensive in the island of Ireland.

When these carriages first came into our possession, however, they had lost all their grandeur, as well as most of their furnishings and fittings but, because they were constructed mainly of quality hardwoods such as teak, oak and mahogany, they were generally structural sound. With our knowledge and research of their original appearance, we have been able to restore them to their original splendour and provide our visitors with an experience of travel as it was one hundred years ago, so different to modern day train travel.

***Above:*** Restoration Work. In addition to capital works, the DARC has been responsible for restoration work to a very high standard, an example of which is GS&WR Carriage No 836, seen here before restoration.

***Above:*** No 836 after restoration.

*Above:* Carriage No 836, newly restored, in April 1998.

*Drew Sucksmith*

*Left and opposite top:* BCDR Composite No 148 under restoration and after entering service.

Restoration is not just confined to vintage carriages. Our more modern carriages also require some degree of restoration to bring them up to the high standard we aim to achieve in our museum. This is necessary to enable us to operate all the various services and events that take place throughout the year, which are essential to produce much needed revenue.

The recent appointment of David Briggs as Carriage and Wagon Officer has greatly strengthened that department. His stamina and enthusiasm know no bounds.

## Labour of love

The first action in any restoration project is that of identification. Each carriage has its own personality and number, and in some cases the vehicle's unique design, such as that of the Royal Saloon, makes its identification obvious.

However, in one case, none of the above clues to identification was present. This was the case with an Ulster Railway carriage in our possession that remained unidentified for a considerable time, despite its most unusual design. It was only with research carried out by the UFTM that its identity and year of construction was established (see chapter 3).

The procedure involved in the restoration of a carriage is to save and record as much information as possible from the carriage before any work begins. Detailed photographs, together with notes, measurements and the retention of sample moulding are essential preliminary tasks. In addition, research is often necessary to obtain information on the many features which have not survived.

Our policy is to repair rather than replace, the aim being to retain as much of the original as possible, bearing in mind that these are intended to be operational carriages and needed to be capable of withstanding continuous use. We do not wish to build a new vehicle but rather to try and retain the personality of the original.

With all the preliminary work complete the task of removal of defective components can begin as well as the labelling and storage of items which are temporarily removed.

Restoration work on the vintage carriages usually involves three distinct 'trades' – mechanical work, joinery work and painting, and is carried out under my direction as Project Leader.

The main elements of joinery work include the repair or replacement of the main structural timbers where necessary, replacement of flooring, external panelling, doors, mouldings, windows, roof covering and internal fittings and finishes. The floor construction of these vintage carriages consisted of two layers of diagonal boarding laid at right angles to each other (double diagonal flooring) which provided a remarkably rigid floor, but modern plywood is an acceptable substitute.

Roofs were originally covered with canvas bedded in white lead paint and finished with a further three coats of white lead. This covering cannot be replicated to-day due to Health and Safety restrictions and, in any case, superior modern roof coverings are now available, which retain the original appearance. The covering used on our most recent restoration project, carriage No 148, was Trocal, a material now widely used on industrial building. Apart from its strength and durability, it can be obtained in white finish which is important for reflecting solar heat.

Internal furnishings and fittings, such as seating, luggage racks, photographs and mirrors, are all carefully researched before installation.

The only other deviation from original practice relates to the external panelling. When originally constructed, the panelling used was 10 mm (⅜") solid mahogany, backed with linen fabric bedded in glue to act as a reinforcement (not 100% satisfactory over 100 years) and prevent the cracking to which this construction was prone. A good modern alternative is 9 mm marine plywood. Modern wbp (water boil proof) plywood is not acceptable.

The mechanical work related to the underframe includes the overhaul of the vacuum brakes, draw gear, bogies and bearings and this is now being carried out by a relatively new member, Bill Brown, whose contribution and enthusiasm has been inspiring.

All this work is a very challenging, but rewarding, activity although some aspects can be very tedious. For example, carriage No 148 had 14 doors, each requiring substantial repairs. In addition, each door had a lock and handle, all of which required the fabrication of new parts. This was very labour intensive requiring many hours work. The only solution was for me to take them home and work on them as time permitted.

Painting and lining is under the control of our professional painter, Cyril Leathers, assisted by Camac Clarke, both volunteers from our early days. In order to achieve the standard of paint finish that these carriages were accustomed to in their early days, great care and attention has to be paid to the preparation. This is a very laborious and time consuming occupation, but the result justifies the effort. The quality of finish is equal to that found in the more established museums and is appreciated by most of our visitors.

Most of the small band of volunteers[3] who have worked on the restoration of our first two projects, carriages Nos 836 and 148, are still actively involved and have now gained a great deal of useful experience and new skills.

We are very fortunate to have had the assistance and advice of a highly respected authority on the BCDR carriages, Desmond Coakham, particularly in respect of carriage livery and lettering. Desmond sent me photocopies of tracings of carriage lettering which he made soon after the carriages were withdrawn from service over fifty years ago. The notes, relating to colours accompanying the tracings, emphasised the care and trouble taken by the draftsmen of the Victorian/Edwardian era and were most helpful in achieving an authentic restoration.

What has been described, relates to only one aspect of restoration undertaken by our volunteers. Other examples include our steam and diesel locomotives, steam crane, Travelling Post Office, Dining Saloon, wagons, signal box, signals, water tower, porters' handcarts, platform furnishings and enamel advertising signs.

Unfortunately, space does not allow me to develop our restoration projects in further detail, except to say that a lot of effort, time and enthusiasm have been expended over the years by so many volunteers.

**Footnotes**

1   NIMC Grants, Appendix 11

2   Norman Bodel, David Briggs, Colin Holiday, Cyril Leathers, Norman Parker, Barry White.

3   Bill Broom, Camac Clarke, Gerry Cochrane, Ian Davis, Phil Dixon, Edward Duly, Robert Gardiner, Neil Hamilton, Colin Holliday, Cyril Leathers, Mike Maddocks, Alan Major, Arthur Muskett, the late Peter Mutton, John McCutcheon.

## CHAPTER 11
# THE GREAT FIRE

Towards the end of 2002, a great effort was made by a number of our volunteers when they embarked on a makeover to the station booking hall to enhance the Edwardian image. As described already in chapter six, financial restrictions had resulted in very limited finishes to the station when first built, which did not create the atmosphere that our mission statement set out to achieve. Concrete block walls, plain tongue and groove boarding to the ceiling gave a very austere appearance and a decision was made to try to improve this.

Under the leadership of one of our young and enthusiastic volunteers, Robert Gardiner, and after extensive research with particular reference to the BCDR station in Saintfield, County Down, a scheme was produced that would encapsulate the essential elements of the period.

The work involved sheeting the walls with tongue and groove boarding, including all the various mouldings, ie dados, skirtings and architraves, which would have been correct for that time. As these mouldings were such a dominant feature it was important to replace them with profiles as close to the original design as possible. Unfortunately, 150 years later these items were now no longer in production. However, this minor difficulty was to be eventually overcome by the enthusiasm of those involved.

The opportunity arose when a house of the correct period in Donaghadee was being renovated and the architraves became available to us. An interesting coincidence was that the former owner of the house was the grandson of WF Minnis, the General Manager of the BCDR.

Similar trouble was taken over the sourcing of authentic light fittings, which were only acquired after many hours searching the whole of County Down for anything that could be used in the restoration.

A big drive was made to have the work completed before the Halloween weekend, one of our major visitor occasions, which we always celebrate at the end of October. This entailed very intensive work into the wee small hours during the final week, by both Robert and his father, whom he had also enlisted. Eventually, all the work, with the exception of the painting, was completed with just one day to spare. The new, transformed booking hall was very much admired and greatly appreciated by all our visitors.

With the Christmas operating season now on the horizon, it was decided to postpone further work until the New Year. The painting preparation would be arranged during the first days of the New Year.

## Shattered dreams

Just after Christmas day, on the morning of 26 December, we felt the world had ended. It is difficult to describe the shock and disbelief felt, when I heard the terrible news that the station building had been gutted by fire in the early hours of the morning. I had been discharged from hospital the previous day, having had a knee operation and was relaxing in bed, when my wife rushed into the room at eight-thirty that morning to inform me that the station had been destroyed by fire. "Surely a nightmare" I thought. But reality soon dawned that this was indeed the case and my immediate thought was for all our volunteers who had worked so hard up until a few days previous.

On arrival at the station, the first person whom I met was Robert, standing in a state of total disbelief. I remember trying to console him by assuring him that the building would eventually be restored again, perhaps, even better than ever. Of course I realised this would never be able to

***Above:*** The remains of the Grotto carriage.

what give one heart when all seemed lost. We have always remembered those people and their many kindnesses when we most needed it.

The fire was discovered by a passing police patrol about 2.30 am and they alerted the local fire brigade. When they arrived, they had to call for assistance from Newcastle and Ballynahinch as the fire had taken such a hold. Our General Manager, Edwin Gray arrived on the scene about 3.30 am to be greeted by the sight of an inferno with flames pouring out through the front widows and main door, as well as from the canopy and grotto carriage at the rear. I dread to think how I would have coped with such a frightening and appalling sight. By the time I arrived at mid-morning, the drama was over with just the smell and charred remains to greet me.

Initially, the view was that the fire had started in the Grotto carriage which was parked at the platform, spread to the canopy and then into the booking hall and shop, but the fire investigation team were able to prove that the shop window had been broken from the outside and the fire started in the shop. It then spread into the renovated booking hall and ticket office. It also spread from the booking hall to the platform canopy and then to the Grotto carriage, that was standing at the platform.

The opinion of the police and fire brigade was that the fire had been malicious. This fact was to add to our grief with the thought that somebody would carry out such a senseless attack.

However, as the initial shock began to subside, it became obvious that the situation could have been much worse. The fire had not completely broken through to the first floor although smoke damage was widespread. Fortunately, the roof was unaffected. We clung to these crumbs of comfort and our mood began to become more up-beat. In no time we were discussing revised operating plans for St Patrick's Day. The fact that the building structure was insured was small comfort, as the contents and the Grotto carriage were not. I was rather shocked to be told that if the fire had started in the Grotto carriage, the station building insurance would not have covered us. Fortunately, our important records and documents had already been contained in a fireproof safe and so remained unaffected.

From an operational point of view, the practical problems of being without our station building and the Grotto carriage were a great nuisance, to put it mildly but, like

replace his personal contribution but it was all that could be said at the time.

A few volunteers had begun the dispiriting task of trying to salvage those exhibits that had survived the flames, although some were badly affected by smoke damage.

It was very heartening to see so many concerned individuals, in addition to our volunteers, who had begun to gather when the news spread. Local councillors, businessmen and individual members of the public all went out of their way to express their profound sympathy and support. The expressions of sympathy and offers of help were such that we were quite amazed to discover that our organisation was held in such high regard in the community. During the weeks which followed, we discovered that local schools, clubs, the fire service and many other organisations and local businesses promoted fund-raising activities to assist with the reinstatement of the station. Such fine actions are

many businesses in this situation, temporary provision had to be accepted. One particular irritating consequence of all the publicity was a reduction in our visitor numbers during the following year, as apparently many people thought that we had been put out of business.

We were impressed with the quick response from DDC staff in organising the securing of the building and engaging a firm of industrial cleaners to remove all the debris in preparation for the reinstatement of the building and canopy. This included the appointment of a Quantity Surveyor to prepare a detailed schedule of work to be agreed with the insurance company, before competitive tenders could be invited. I was asked to provide copies of my original drawings of the station, together with detailed information on the recent work carried out to the booking hall.

We took the opportunity to include additional work (at our own expense) in the reinstatement contract, which would add further additional Edwardian details, such as ceiling mouldings and double doors, as well as side screens at the platform entrance.

Also included, was the replacement of the concrete pavers to the floor of the booking hall with genuine Edwardian diamond patterned blue quarry tiles that had been salvaged from Coleraine station platform. Although these were backed with old cement, which had to be laboriously removed by hand, a slow process which came close to delaying the contract and upsetting the contractor, it was well worth the trouble because the finished floor now gives the appearance of having been laid in 1859.

A further consequence of this incident was the loss of our Santa's Grotto accommodation. This had been a 60-foot carriage, fitted out with two grottos and elaborate circulation corridors to disguise the double presence of the great man. Special lighting and sound effects, together with the traditional Christmas decorations, had transformed this carriage into a childrens' wonderland.

*Above:* TPO carriage restored, incorporating Grotto facilities.

As the facilities provided in this carriage were also required for the Halloween event, now just nine months away, urgent action was needed to provide a replacement. We had two options:

1   Accept a generous offer of NCC carriage No 411 from the RPSI. This would involve transportation costs and an extra carriage would take up valuable space on our already overcrowded track.

2   Partially convert our existing Travelling Post Office (TPO) carriage, which was quickly deteriorating and unlikely to be restored in the foreseeable future. Two grottos could be provided with minimum alteration to the original interior. The selection of this carriage would insure its immediate restoration.

With the selection of the TPO carriage as the new grotto coach, together with all available hands to the wheel we had grotto facilities restored in time for Halloween and the restoration of the TPO as a bonus.

## Hard times

The loss of the station building also had an immediate effect on the comforts of the volunteers, who were now without their mess room. We had to set up camp in the un-heated workshop for the foreseeable future – not a pleasant experience in the middle of January.

*Above:* Temporary mess facilities in the workshop.

***Above:*** Re-opening after the fire, in September 2003, with Walter Love doing the honours alongside No 3.

Thankfully, all the disruption to train services and amenities eventually came to an end in September 2003, when the renovated station building was formally reopened by Radio Ulster's Walter Love. This was a great occasion for rejoicing with all our friends and supporters and, in particular, the officers and councillors of DDC who supported us so well at a time of trauma. They say that it's an ill wind that blows no good. How true in this instance, as the amount of sympathy and goodwill we received was most gratifying. It was marked shortly afterwards by DDC awarding us a very timely grant which, up to this point, had been looking extremely doubtful.

# CHAPTER 12

# CONCLUSION

I've now reached the end of this journey, spurred on by being asked questions about the early period in our development ,as well as comments from well-meaning individuals telling me "You better get it down on paper before it's too late!"

There have been many difficulties in getting to this stage, in particular trying to stimulate my memory of so many events since 1982, deciding which of them to include and which to leave out. There was an added difficulty of trying not to get too technical in my descriptions of carriages, etc, while at the same time keeping in mind the fact that, for many readers, it was precisely this sort of detail which would interest them. I hope I have succeeded in attaining a reasonable balance. I have also strived to present the facts as accurately as I can remember them. No doubt some may disagree with a few of my more personal comments on events but it is for them to give their own account.

To the question which I have constantly asked myself along the way, "Why are you doing this?", I can honestly say it has given me much reward and satisfaction, not least to see the degree of enjoyment and pleasure experienced by our many volunteers. This applies in particular to our older members, some of whom are now in their eighties, still active and making a significant contribution.

I'm also aware that this organisation has brought together people from all walks of life, backgrounds and traditions, working together to achieve a common goal. In many cases lasting friendships have been established.

Looking back over the years of hard work and struggle, it is comforting to think that we have succeeded in saving much of the local railway heritage of the steam age which would otherwise have been lost.

Perhaps it is also worth noting that, although there have been many high points over the years, there also have been moments of frustration, disappointment and setback, the most pronounced of these being the unsuccessful bid in 1996 for a HLF grant for a Carriage Display Gallery.

Personnel problems, too, sapped my energy during my period as General Manager. I came to realise that this was inevitable, given the diverse opinions and characters involved, all with an overriding passion to see the project succeed but with different ideas as to how this could be achieved.

The first such incident I well remember concerned two of our Directors, one quite young, the other a more mature member. I can't recall the cause of the clash, which disturbed me at the time, but now in retrospect seems quite hilarious and worth recounting.

A group of us had been working quite hard off-site all day at some heavy task and had returned to our depot at Downpatrick. It was late evening, dark and about six of us were gathered together in our little wooden hut for a well-deserved cup of tea, to mull over the day's events. Everything was peaceful and quiet and a single candle provided a relaxing atmosphere. Only the scurrying of rats outside disturbed the calm.

Suddenly, this relaxed atmosphere was shattered by the noise of hurried footsteps outside on the gravel as someone approached our hut with unusual haste. The door was flung open, almost extinguishing our candle as our junior director burst in. He slammed the door and put his back against it to prevent his pursuer from following. After gulping for breath he panted, "He's going to kill me!" The 'he' in question was our more mature director, still lurking outside somewhere in the dark. I never did find out what had caused this episode but I'm glad to say it couldn't have been too serious because they're both still with us.

Since 1982, when I first embarked on the scheme, I have felt the strain of the constant responsibility for the task I had set in motion. This responsibility grew heavier as the years passed, as I was aware of the amount of public money and time invested by so many influential people. I did of course have strong support from a marvellous and most competent Board of Directors and Management Committee but, having started down this road, I felt the onus was on me not to let everyone down.

On reflection, a lot of this worry was due to over-sensitivity on my part, coupled by some feelings of doubt that we could handle a project which seemed to grow day by day. It is well to remember that most of us were still in full-time employment at the time and getting the railway off the ground was a spare-time activity.

While thoroughly enjoying what I was doing, the effect on my health would eventually take its toll and I decided to retire from all major decision making in 2004. I am now taking it a little easier, happily concentrating on vintage carriage restoration, an occupation I'd strongly recommend to anyone looking for relaxing occupational therapy.

However, these feelings are not the overriding ones. Looking around me now I get a great sense of personal achievement, proud that Downpatrick has now got a wonderful tourist attraction and I will be always deeply grateful to those many, wonderful people who believed in the project and strove so hard to see it through.

It can be safely said that the Downpatrick & County Down Railway is now firmly established with immense potential for future development and success.

***Above left:*** Inch Abbey station on St Patrick's Day 2008, showing the run-round loop and coaching stock at the new bay platform.

*Norman Johnston*

***Above right:*** Two locomotives, RPSI 0-6-0ST No 3 and 0-6-0T No 90 at Inch Abbey.

*George Walker*

***Bottom left:*** 0-6-0T No 90 pauses between duties at Downpatrick on 17 March 2008. The unrestored SLNCR railcar is on the right.

*Norman Johnston*

# Appendix 1

## REVIEW OF MUSEUMS IN NORTHERN IRELAND
by a Working Party (1983)

### A NEW CULTURAL INITIATIVE FOR NORTHERN IRELAND

*The Museums and Galleries Commission, in a Report issued today, state that museum provision in Northern Ireland lags sadly behind the rest of the United Kingdom. They propose expenditure of £1 million a year to bring Northern Ireland into line with museum services elsewhere in the United Kingdom. Both central government and local authorities will be required to raise £1/2 million a year to implement the report's recommendations. The £1 million will be to foster museum growth outside Belfast. The Report states bluntly that new industries will not be attracted t Northern Ireland if it is culturally deprived.*

*The Report recommends a complete merger between the Ulster Museum and the Ulster Folk and Transport museum to create a new National Museum of Ulster comparable with any of the national museums in London, Edinburgh or Cardiff.*

*It also recommends the setting up of an Area Museums Service to foster the existing museums outside Belfast and to plan new ones. The Report praises the initiative of Downpatrick, Enniskillen, Fermanagh, Lisburn Londonderry and elsewhere, and recommends that considerable government funds should be forthcoming to enable capital development to take place there. The Report........*

The following is an extract from the Report:-

2.32 *The Downpatrick and Ardglass Railway Society has drawn up a scheme to restore and operate the old 9-mile Ardglass Branch Line from Downpatrick as a Working Railway Museum at a total cost of £500,000.*

*Planning to date has been carried out by a Steering Committee under the chairmanship of Mr.E.P.G.Cochrane, R.I.B.A. It is intended to establish the museum as a private trust, and advice is being taken with a view to forming a private limited liability company to operate the railway. There is a feasibility study for the first phase of the scheme to restore about one mile of track and buildings associated with the railway. The cost is estimated at about £30,000 a year over three years. Some initial clearing has already taken place. Much of the work can be done with ACE[1] labour and most of the land over which the track passes has been donated to the scheme.*

*The Second Phase to extend the track another two miles to Ballynoe is estimated at a cost of £89,000 in one year, and the Third Phase to cover the last 6 miles to Ardglass is estimated at £358,300 over seven years.*

*It is planned to re-erect a railway station next to the new car park which will also serve visitors to Down Museum. Plans include an exhibition gallery, in the station building for the display of an extensive collection of photographs, models and small exhibits already in existence.*

*The Society hopes that consideration will be given to the suggestion that the Ulster Folk and Transport Museum's Railway Collection[2] could be accommodated in the Downpatrick –Ardglass scheme. This would allow exhibits to be displayed in working condition on the track.*

1   Action for Community Employment
    (90% government grant-aided)
2   Currently in Witham Street

# Appendix 2

## GRANTS FROM NORTHERN IRELAND MUSEUMS COUNCIL
## 1994-2008

| Collections Care | | | | |
|---|---|---|---|---|
| **Year** | **Project** | **Grant Offered** | **%** | **Amount spent** |
| 1995-96 | Conservation of steam crane and tenders | £3,000 | 40% | £2,919.83 |
| 1995-96 | Purchase of fire-proof records cabinet | £400 | 58% | £343.00 |
| 1997-98 | Refurbishment of carriage | £1,314 | 57% | £1,314.00 |
| 1998-99 | Refit of carriage to meet Health & Safety standards | £3,600 | 75% | £3,579.60 |
| 1998-99 | Purchase of scaffolding tower | £430 | 50% | £430.00 |
| 1999-2000 | Restoration of railway carriage | £4,000 | 55% | £4,000.00 |
| 2000-01 | Restoration of railway carriage | £4,594 | 50% | £4,594.00 |
| 2002-03 | Railway carriage roof conservation | £2,877 | 50% | £2,877.00 |
| 2003-04 | Restoration of TPO carriage | £4,977 | 50% | £4,339.00 |
| 2005-06 | CCTV system | £4,165 | 65% | £4,135.00 |
| 2006-07 | Care and display of archive holdings | £800 | 65% | £781.90 |
| 2007-08 | Environmental monitoring equipment | £534 | 65% | £505.70 |

| Use of Collections/ Access and interpretation | | | | |
|---|---|---|---|---|
| **Year** | **Project** | **Grant Offered** | **%** | **Amount spent** |
| 1996-97 | Improvement to visitor access to toilets | £2,458 | 50% | £2,458 |
| 1997-98 | Information panels and signage | £675 | 75% | £675 |
| 1997-98 | Information leaflets | £600 | 75% | £600 |
| 1999-2000 | Promotional leaflet | £515 | 50% | £360 |
| 2000-01 | Eight interpretation panels | £219 | 50% | £219 |
| 2000-01 | Improvements to exhibition, displays and storage | £1,706 | 50% | £1,706 |
| 2003-04 | Window security | £622 | 50% | £622 |
| 2004-05 | Promotional material | £540 | 50% | £425 |

| Specimen Purchase Scheme | | | | |
|---|---|---|---|---|
| **Year** | **Project** | **Grant Offered** | **%** | **Amount spent** |
| 1994-95 | Steam crane and tender | £212.77 | 50% | £212.77 |
| 1996-97 | Railway carriage underframe | £188 | 75% | £188 |
| 1997-98 | Royal Saloon carriage underframe | £375 | 50% | £375 |
| 2000-01 | Transport of passenger brake carriage | £794.50 | 50% | £794.50 |
| 2000-01 | Transport of RB3 railbus | £519 | 50% | £519 |

# Appendix 3

## STOCK LIST

| LOCOMOTIVES | | | | | |
|---|---|---|---|---|---|
| | **Built** | **Acquired** | **Owner** | **Status** | **Comments** |
| | | | | | |
| Orenstein & Koppel No 1 | 1934 | 1987 | ISCLG* | Under restoration | Built in Berlin for Irish Sugar Co |
| Orenstein & Koppel No 3 | 1935 | 1987 | ISCLG* | Operational | Built in Berlin for Irish Sugar Co |
| GS&WR 0-6-0T No 90 | 1875 | 2008 | Irish Rail | Operational | Oldest Operating Steam Loco in Ireland |
| CIÉ Maybach No 421 | 1962 | 1986 | DCDR | Operational | |
| CIÉ Maybach No 432 | 1963 | 1986 | DCDR | In store | |
| CIÉ Deutz No 611 | 1961 | 1996 | ITG | Operational | |
| CIÉ Deutz No 613 | 1961 | 1989 | Private | Operational | |
| CIÉ Deutz No 617 | 1961 | 1995 | ITG | Operational | |
| BR Leyland Railbus RB3 | 1981 | 2001 | NIR | Operational | |
| SLNCR Railcar B | 1947 | | DCDR | In store | In very poor condition |
| | | | *\* Irish Sugar Co Locomotive Group* | | |

| WAGONS | | | | | |
|---|---|---|---|---|---|
| | | | | | |
| UTA open wagon | | 1985 | DCDR | Operational | First exhibit |
| Courtaulds open wagon | | | DCDR | Operational | |
| GNR cement van | 1900? | 1998 | DCDR | Under restoration | Typical pre-First World War van |
| CIÉ van No 18885 | | | DCDR | Operational | |
| LMS NCC brown vans (4) | | 1987 | DCDR | In store | Purchased for underframes |
| GNR(I) bogie 'P' van 619 | 1934 | 1987 | DCDR | Underframe/153 | Purchased for underframes |
| GNR brake van No 2053 | | 1987 | DCDR | Operational | Our first passenger vehicle |
| GS&WR ballast plough No 8452 | | 1990 | Westrail | Operational | Used in construction of Inch Branch |
| GS&WR ballast wagons Nos 8314, 8411 | | 1986 | DCDR | Operational | Used in construction of Inch Branch |
| NIR hopper No C496 | | | DCDR | Operational | Bogie wagon |
| Oil tanker No 1536 | 1922 | 1999 | DCDR | Operational | |

## MISCELLANEOUS

| | Built | Acquired | Owner | Status | Comments |
|---|---|---|---|---|---|
| LMS NCC steam crane No 3084 | 1931 | 1994 | DCDR | | Built by Cowans Sheldon & Co |
| NIR hedge cutter No HC1 | | | DCDR | | |
| Tamping machine | 1978 | 2008 | DCDR | Under restoration | |
| Wickham inspection vehicle | | 1998 | ITG | In store | |
| Wickham inspection vehicle | | | Private | Under restoration | |

## CARRIAGES

| | | | | | |
|---|---|---|---|---|---|
| BCDR No 39 | 1903 | 1987 | DCDR | In store | 6-wheel brake built in Queen's Quay |
| BCDR No 148 | 1897 | 1988 | DCDR | Operational | Half 148/half 152 |
| BCDR No 153 | 1897 | 1984 | DCDR | In store | Royal Saloon built by Ashbury |
| BCDR No 154 | 1918 | 1986 | DCDR | In store | 6-wheel second |
| BCDR No 2 Railmotor | 1905 | 1985 | DCDR | Under restoration | Built by Metropolitan, Birmingham |
| GNR No ? | ? | 1993 | DCDR | In store | 6-wheel third |
| UR | 1862 | 1986 | DCDR | In store | 4-wheel family saloon |
| GS&WR No 69 | 1888 | 1992 | Private | Under restoration | Full brake now family saloon |
| GS&WR No 836 | 1902 | 1986 | DCDR | Operational | Third Dublin/Cork Express |
| GS&WR No 1097 | 1923 | 2005 | RPSI | Operational | Side corridor Tri-compo |
| GS&WR No 1287 | 1915 | 2004 | RPSI | In store | Tri-compo – mess accommodation |
| MGWR | 1894 | 2006 | DCDR | In store | 6-wheel |
| MGWR | 1892 | 2006 | DCDR | In store | 6-wheel |
| CIÉ No 1918 (orig 2163) | 1957 | 1988 | DCDR | Static use | Open Brake Standard (orig compo) |
| CIÉ No 1944 | 1956 | 1995 | DCDR | In store | Park Royal Brake Standard |
| CIÉ No 2419 | 1956 | 1988 | DCDR | Operational | Buffet Car |
| CIÉ No 3223 | 1954 | 1988 | DCDR | Operational | Open Standard Steam Generating |
| CIÉ No 2978 | 1958 | 1995 | DCDR | Operational | TPO; Current use – grotto carriage |
| NIR No 728 (orig UTA 306) | 1951 | 1991 | DCDR | Operational | 70-class trailer; currently a Club Car |
| NIR No 713 (orig NCC 66) | 1924 | 1991 | DCDR | | Grotto Carriage. Destroyed 2002 |

# Bibliography

Coakham DG, Passenger Stock of the BCDR (*Journal of the Irish Railway Record Society* Volume 7)

Patterson EM, *The Belfast & County Down Railway* (David & Charles)

Grenfell Morton, *Railways in Ulster* (Friar's Bush Press)

*Down Recorder* (various issues)

*Mourne Observer* (various issues)

*Down Democrat* (various issues)

*Belfast Telegraph* (various issues)

*News Letter* (various issues)

***Above:*** Orenstein & Koppel 0-4-0T No 3 passes the Home Junction as it approaches Downpatrick on 16 July 2006.

*Wilson Adams*

# Index